BEING
HAPPY
IN AN
UNHAPPY
WORLD

JOHN HAGEE

John Hagee Ministries
P.O. Box 1400
San Antonio, TX 78295-1400
(210) 494-3900

First Printing, June 1989
Second Printing, May 1990
Third Printing, October 1993
Fourth Printing, April 1994
Fifth Printing, February 1995
Sixth Printing, February 1999

*This book is dedicated to my
beloved father, Rev. Bythel Hagee of Houston,
Texas, an anointed preacher of the gospel, a faithful
servant of Jesus Christ, who passed away while
this manuscript was being written.*

Contents

1

The Pursuit of Happiness

The Constitution of the United States guarantees its citizens the right to "life, liberty and the pursuit of happiness." But you don't need a Phi Beta Kappa key to know that Americans aren't happy.

We represent six percent of the world's population and take ninety percent of the world's tranquilizers. The message? We're uptight. As one lady said, "The only thing holding me together is my hair spray."

What about you? Do you say:

• your birthday cake collapsed from the weight of the candles?

• you sunk your teeth into a sandwich and they stayed there?

- your back goes out more often than you do?
- all the names in your little black book belong to doctors?
- you called Suicide Prevention and they put you on hold?

This Is Happiness?

Twentieth-century man wakes up in the morning to the clatter of an alarm clock. He leaps out of bed knowing he must shower, shave and scramble out of the door in twenty minutes to beat the bumper-to-bumper traffic on the freeway.

He climbs into his clothes and hurries down the hall to the kitchen, where he pours a cup of coffee into his spill-proof cup. He squirms into the bucket seat of his sports car and plunges into traffic at breakneck speed, bobbing and weaving through the maze of metal, honking his horn and squealing his tires when the light turns green.

When our hero arrives at the office, he searches for a parking place, then waits impatiently for an elevator that arrives already full. Stumbling up seven flights of stairs, he flops down at his desk like a gored matador, ready at last to face the challenges of the day.

This is happiness?

What *Is* Happiness?

Americans are pursuing happiness frantically. Something to swallow. Something to sniff. Something to smoke. Something to spend money on. The search for happiness itself winds up being one of the chief causes of *un*happiness.

The more knowledge we acquire, the less wisdom we seem to have. The more economic security we attain, the more corruption we generate. The more pleasure we enjoy, the more disenchanted we become with ourselves, our spouses, our children and our destiny.

What is happiness?

The sick man would say happiness is health. The ambitious man would say happiness is success. The poor man would say happiness is wealth. The scholar would say happiness is learning. And the poor rascal whose story we recounted at the beginning of this chapter would no doubt say happiness is rest and relaxation. But none of these things produces lasting happiness.

Where Is Happiness to Be Found?

Not in unbelief. Voltaire was an infidel of international notoriety. In the twilight hours of his life he wrote, "I wish I had never been born."

Not in pleasure. Lord Byron lived a life of uninterrupted sensual stimulation. In the end his gifted pen recorded, "The worm, the canker and grief are mine alone."

Not in money. Jay Gould, the millionaire, had enormous wealth. As he lay dying, his tortured lips whispered, "I suppose I am the most miserable man on earth."

Not in success. Alexander the Great had subjugated every known kingdom on earth by the age of thirty-three. How did he respond? He wept in his tent, crying, "There are no worlds left to conquer."

Happiness Is Not Haphazard

Happiness may be sought, thought or caught—but never bought. A lot of happiness is overlooked because it doesn't cost anything. The happiest people are those who are too busy to notice whether they are happy or not. If you can't find happiness along the way, you'll never find it at the end of the road.

Happiness is not haphazard. It doesn't come our way by accident. People who think happiness is accidental, that it drops out of the sky like rain, forget that even rain is not accidental. It is given by the hand of God.

The Divine Spark

Man's unhappiness lies in his potential greatness, in the divine dimension of his nature. The divine spark within us is both the secret of our progress and the source of our problem.

A cow is satisfied to chew her cud. A dog is satisfied to gnaw his meatless bone. A bird is satisfied with last year's dried nest.

Not so with man. Nothing that comes from the outside can satisfy the soul on the inside. Happiness is not something we carry in our hands. It's something we carry in our hearts. The Scottish poet Robert Burns wrote:

> If happiness hath not her seat
>   and center in the breast
> We may be wise, or rich, or great,
>   but never can be blest.

The Magna Carta of Happiness

The greatest formula for happiness ever invented was spoken into existence by a Jewish rabbi who lived almost two thousand years ago. It teaches not only the deepest of spiritual truths but also practical principles by which anyone can find happiness, health, success and tranquility: peace of mind and peace of soul. It is better known as Jesus' Sermon on the Mount, which begins with a series of intriguing—and astonishing—statements about where happiness is to be found. These principles of happiness are widely known as the beatitudes.

Why are so many of us leading lives of misery and despair? Because we are ignoring—or rejecting—the only reliable formula for happiness. Jesus' principles of happiness are a cool, refreshing spring in a dry place, a rock of refuge in a weary land.

Happiness Here and Now

The time to be happy is now. The place to be happy is right where you are. I invite you to join me, through the following chapters, on a journey in search of happiness in an unhappy world. We will explore the "Magna Carta of Happiness" and discover that happiness comes not from what you have, but from what you are.

But first—lest we hang on to any futile and destructive illusions—let's get crystal clear on some of the places where happiness is not found.

2

Where Not to Find Happiness

We all pursue happiness. It comes naturally. The problem is that we keep looking for it in all the wrong places. In this chapter I'd like to point out just a few of the places where happiness is not to be found.

HAPPINESS IS NOT FOUND IN RELIGION

I know it sounds shocking for a preacher to say so, but the fact is that happiness is not found in religion.

Now we need to distinguish between being religious and being spiritual. Religion is nothing more than a pretense of godliness held together with the glue of idolatry, ritual rules and the traditions of men.

Ritual Without Righteousness

Religion is form without force. It is ceremony without change in conduct or character. It thrives on human traditions that exclude the commandments of God.

The Pharisees were extremely religious. They kept all their self-inflicted religious rules but had hearts like granite. They were cold, loveless, mean-spirited, Scripture-quoting alligators. They were unforgiving legalists. Some, it is said, even carried swords and would hack you to death (in love, of course, and to the glory of God!) if you disputed their doctrine.

They attended worship faithfully—but only to be seen by men. They prayed long, loud, pious prayers—but only in places where others would hear them. They gave up to a third of their income to the temple—and every shekel was given with the sound of trumpets for personal recognition. Jesus did not consider their ritual a substitute for righteousness:

> For I tell you that unless your righteousness surpasses that of the Pharisees and the teachers of the law, you will certainly not enter the kingdom of heaven (Matt. 5:20).

Tradition: the Religious Rut

Religion is rich in tradition but poverty-stricken where love, joy and peace are concerned. Tradition is a religious rut. Ruts are easy to follow, but you can only go where others have gone. What if God wants to do a new work in your life? If you're stuck in a rut, you'll miss it.

Tradition holds on to the past. It resists change. But the path that leads to spiritual maturity, and to happiness, demands change.

When Jesus healed the man with the withered hand on the Sabbath, the enraged Pharisees approached Him, fists clenched, teeth grinding, screaming, "We have a tradition! You can't heal on the Sabbath!" In their religiosity, they were prepared to let the man remain crippled just to preserve their tradition. Jesus said, "Why do you break the command of God for the sake of your tradition?" (Matt. 15:3).

Tradition stunts spiritual growth. It destroys the adventure of faith. It squashes the fresh move of the Holy Spirit. It produces immature saints who become diaper dictators with pablum personalities.

Legalism Terminates Joy

A young girl was visiting her holier-than-thou aunt in the country for the summer. The woman's legalistic attitude was constantly in evidence. Every time the little girl wanted to do something, the woman would say, "Don't do that," or "You can't do that."

One day the little girl was walking down the road and came upon a long-faced mule near the fence. She walked over, patted it on the head, and said, "Don't feel bad, Mr. Mule. My aunt has religion, too."

Religion is intolerant of those who don't fit our form. Our attitudes of intolerance are manifested in sustained stares or caustic comments. Such religious reactions will destroy churches faster than a five-alarm fire. Paul rebuked the Galatians thoroughly for deserting Christ (Gal. 1:6), for setting aside the grace of God (2:21) and for becoming bewitched by legalism (3:1).

Pharisees Are Never Happy

Jesus reserved His most scathing remarks not for struggling sinners but for religious legalists who pursued a form of godliness while denying the power of God. They were pompous peacocks, hypocrites and glory-hogs who had an inner compulsion to be the center of attention. Their descendants are still with us.

If there is something within you that instinctively criticizes people who do not fit your mold; something that compels you to look down your nose at those who disagree with you; a compulsion for having your talents and accomplishments on display at all times—you are in danger of becoming a modern-day Pharisee. And Pharisees are never happy.

The Idolatry of Stubbornness

Religion is saturated with idolatry. The first commandment God gave Moses—the top priority on God's agenda—was that Israel should never make a graven image resembling any creature on earth, in the heavens or in the seas. God promised that His judgment would fall upon any person who bowed down in any form of worship to these idols. His judgment would also fall upon their children through future generations (see Ex. 20:3-5). Idolatry is spiritual adultery and God hates it.

Many church members today are bound by idolatry. I'm not talking about idols of wood and stone. I'm talking about idols of thought and opinion. The Bible says, "Rebellion is as the sin of witchcraft, and stubbornness is as iniquity and idolatry" (1 Sam. 15:23, KJV).

There is a divine equation here. Stubbornness is tantamount to idolatry.

A stubborn man is one who will not change his mind even when God's Word says he is wrong. He has made an idol of his opinion. He will not change his lukewarm commitment to Christ even though the Bible says, "Love the Lord your God with all your heart and with all your soul and with all your strength" (Deut. 6:5). He will not change his stewardship of his money even when the Bible declares, "Will a man rob God? Yet you rob me...Bring the whole tithe into the storehouse" (Mal. 3:8,10).

When your thoughts and opinions become intellectual gods in rebellion against the Word of God, you are in idolatry. How can you be happy in that condition?

Creeds Without Christ

A man in a rural church was brought before the discipline board for conduct unbecoming of a Christian. He looked the elders straight in the eye and said, "Brothers, I have stolen cows. I have stolen hogs and chickens and eggs. I have even stolen from the offering plate as it came by in church. But I want you to know I never lost my religion." It's true. You can say the Apostles' Creed and still be a thief.

Religion substitutes ceremony for genuine change in conduct and character. The word "religion" comes from the Latin *religio*, which means "to tie men back to God." Jesus Christ is the only One who can tie a man or woman back to God. It can never be accomplished through creeds, ceremonies or chants. Creeds without Christ are as sounding brass and tinkling cymbals.

God Wants Us to Change

Jesus demanded change in the lives of the people to whom He ministered. When the Pharisees caught the woman in the act of adultery (doesn't it make you wonder where they were and what they were doing, to catch her in the act?), they piously paraded her before Jesus, demanding that she be stoned to death on the spot. Their loveless religiosity sought only punishment.

But Jesus sought restoration. After He dismissed the Pharisees, He forgave the woman. And He added, "Go now and leave your life of sin'' (John 8:11).

Greasy Grace

The message? God expects us to change. There are predators in the pulpit proclaiming a gospel of greasy grace and gospel lace. "You don't need to change" is their message. It's a fraud. Jesus did not teach that. Neither did Paul. We preach and teach it because it sedates our consciences. It allows our carnal and godless lives to be ruled by the world, the flesh and the devil.

But to extend forgiveness without demanding change is to make the grace of God an accomplice to evil. It is to give the offender a license to sin. Religion says, "No change is necessary." The Bible says, "Have nothing to do with the fruitless deeds of darkness, but rather expose them" (Eph. 5:11).

The Religious Mask

Many people wear a religious mask, pretending to be more spiritual than they are. They walk into the sanctuary stiffly, their noses tilted slightly upward. If it rained, these stuffed shirts would drown. The joy of fellowship is fractured by the judgmental attitude and the critical look of these pompous peacocks.

I have told my congregation, "If you're going to sin, sin big. Pull out the stops! Live like hell—so when you get there you won't wonder why. At least you won't be a smug, self-righteous hypocrite, professing Christ without possessing Christ!"

Fruit of the Spirit

Happiness is not found in religion. It is found in a life-changing relationship with Jesus Christ, where "if anyone

20

is in Christ, he is a new creation; the old has gone, the new has come!'' (2 Cor. 5:17).

Happiness is a result of the indwelling of the Holy Spirit. "The fruit of the Spirit," Paul says, "is love, joy, peace, patience, kindness, goodness, faithfulness, gentleness and self-control" (Gal. 5:22-23).

Fruit is the product of the tree. Happiness is the product of the Spirit of God. If you want your life to be flooded with old-fashioned, simple-hearted, overflowing happiness, then be filled with the Spirit of the living God.

HAPPINESS IS NOT FOUND IN THE GOLDEN RULE

I hate to keep rattling your teacup, but did you know that the Golden Rule is a fraud? That's right. Without the character of Christ in the life of the person quoting the rule, there is no greater fraud on the face of the earth.

The drunk who buys a drink for another drunk is practicing the Golden Rule without the character of Christ. He is doing for another what he wishes others would do for him: help him get drunk. Likewise, the drug addict sharing a fix with another addict is practicing the Golden Rule without the character of Christ. And so on.

"Do to others as you would have them do to you" (Luke 6:31). There are three words that help us capture the essence of this verse and prevent its fraudulent misuse: desire, deeds and duty.

Desire and Disqualification

Many people let lack of desire disqualify them from happiness. They won't participate in the game of life. They'd rather sit in the dugout and pout. Why? Because they don't know the right people. Or they aren't educated enough. Or others have gotten all the breaks in life.

I went to college with a young man who had a severe case of multiple sclerosis. His every exertion required excruciating effort. He couldn't write because his hands were twisted and inflexible, so he tape-recorded the lectures and committed them to memory. He was never late for class, and he never complained.

He graduated with honors, then went on to earn advanced degrees in order to help other people who considered themselves handicapped. The thought that *he* was handicapped never entered his mind. He didn't disqualify himself from the game of life. He chose to play it with enthusiasm.

"There Is No Junk Here"

Some disqualify themselves from happiness out of an exaggerated sense of weakness. They feel they have so little to give that they give nothing at all.

When I was in Bible college, I went to the junkyard one day looking for an inexpensive spare tire for my already nearly comatose car.

"May I help you?" asked the owner.

"I'm looking for a junk tire to use for a spare," I replied.

"There are no junk tires here," he said. "There are no junk bumpers and no junk hubcaps, either. In fact, nothing here is junk."

"All right," I responded sportingly. "Then what do you call this ocean of unclaimed blessing covered with rust?"

"Son, you need to understand something," the man countered. "Junk is something that has no value. Something that cannot contribute anything to anybody, ever. Junk is that which has absolutely nothing to give. As long as it has something to give, it's not junk."

I never forgot that lesson. A person only becomes junk when he refuses to contribute to anyone or anything. As long as there is something to give yourself to, there is hope of happiness.

Too Good to Give?

On the other end of the spectrum there are those who refuse to participate in the game of life not because they have too little to give, but because they feel they have too much. These superior souls won't even join the team because the other players are so inferior. They won't join the church because the church isn't perfect. They won't sing in the choir because the conductor's musical training is inadequate. Can you see how completely these poor people cut themselves off from happiness?

Taking Responsibility

Our deeds are a reflection of our desires, which reflect our character. We and we alone are responsible for our deeds. There comes a time in the life of each one of us when we must assume responsibility for who we are and what we do. We can't blame mother, father, professor, boss, preacher or God.

"If anyone competes as an athlete," Paul wrote, "he does not receive the victor's crown unless he competes according to the rules" (2 Tim. 2:5). Life is controlled by rules. We have to obey the rules or suffer the consequences.

Every game must have rules or it becomes an absurd activity. Playing baseball without rules for how many men can be on a team, or how many strikes a batter gets before he's called out, leads to athletic anarchy. To rebel against the rules leaves the umpire with no alternative but to throw the offender out of the game.

When our deeds violate the rules of the game of life as prescribed by God, the righteous judge, He has no choice but to throw us out of the game. Violating the rules always involves penalties. A rule without a penalty is no rule at all. Happiness is found in keeping the rules.

The darkest days in the history of the people of Israel came when "Israel had no king; everyone did as he saw fit" (Judg. 17:6). What was the result? It was not a golden age of peace and light. God brought judgment, and it was an age of mud, blood and tears.

Keeping the Rules

When we break the rules, it hurts not only us, but also everyone in our house, our church and our office. I attended college on a football scholarship. I played offensive guard and defensive linebacker. I know about rules and penalties. If I choose to be offside when the ball is snapped, whose business is it but mine? Just because it's the fourth quarter of the championship game, the score is tied and we've got the ball first-and-goal at the two-yard line, whom does it hurt?

Obviously it hurts the whole team. It may cause everyone associated with me to fail to reach a goal we have worked hard to attain. Fifteen years later at the class reunion the members of that team will still be saying, "We might have won the championship if only you had kept the rules."

Hurting Ourselves and Others

How many of America's youth have broken the rules of common sense and good health by taking drugs? How many Americans are dying from AIDS because they broke the rules of God? How many millions of unborn babies have been scrambled to a bloody pulp because someone broke the rules? How many of our children lie dead or maimed beside the highways of America because a drunken driver decided to break the rules?

None of these rule-breakers can confine the consequences

of their actions to themselves alone. Their actions have broken the hearts of countless mothers, fathers, brothers, sisters, children and friends—all of whom must cruelly share in their suffering.

Conscience: God's Watchdog

God has given each of us a conscience that will not be silent when we do wrong. It hits us between the eyes like a sledgehammer and says, You shouldn't have done that. The conscience is an organ of discernment. It helps us discern right from wrong. It is God's watchdog over the soul.

The moment conscience speaks, the carnal mind will try to justify what the conscience condemns. The carnal mind says, Did you see that woman?

Conscience says, Better leave that alone.

The carnal mind fires back, But did you see how she was dressed? Just take one more look.

This is how we argue with ourselves. There is an internal war raging between right and wrong. A war between truth and deception, between honor and dishonor. The voice we listen to represents the power—Christ or Satan—to whom we yield control of our life at that moment.

If we want to be happy, we can't abuse our consciences. It will bark all night and we'll wake up dog tired!

Giving Our All

We not only need to play the game according to the rules, we also need to play it with all our hearts, minds, souls and strength. We must give it our best shot every minute. This is our duty before God, who has given us life—"put us in the game."

Remember the sin of the church in Laodicea? The church didn't walk off the field and quit altogether. It kept playing, but only halfheartedly. John recorded the opinion of our Lord when he wrote, "You are neither cold nor hot. I wish you were either one or the other! So, because you are lukewarm—neither hot nor cold—I am about to spit you out of my mouth" (Rev. 3:15-16). The message? Halfhearted play is disgusting in the eyes of God.

Doing Our Duty

When we stand before the righteous judge, His approval will depend not upon our skill, nor upon our success, but upon our willingness to do our duty. Duty is not what we choose to do; it is what He has chosen for us to do.

It is said that King Henry of Bavaria became weary of court life and decided to enter a monastery. The prior gave him the rules of the order. The king listened eagerly and expressed delight at the prospect of such complete consecration.

The prior explained that obedience, exact and complete, was the first requisite of sainthood. The monarch promised to follow his will in every detail. "Very well, then," said the prior. "Go back to your throne and do your duty in the station God has assigned to you." The king took up his scepter again. Ever after, his subjects said of him, "King Henry has learned to rule by learning to obey."

HAPPINESS IS NOT FOUND IN TOMORROW

Much happiness is assassinated by "waiting for tomorrow." How many times have I heard people postpone the joy of life by saying things like:

"I'll be happy when I get older." Then when they do get older everything hurts—and what doesn't hurt doesn't work!

"I'll be happy when I get married." Then they get married and discover that, although everyone gets married for better or worse, not everyone gets married for good.

"I'll be happy when I have children." Then they have children and discover there are three ways to get something done: do it yourself, hire someone to do it or forbid your kids to do it.

"I'll be happy when I retire." Then they find out that the only bad thing about doing nothing is that you never get a day off.

Life on "Someday I'll"

The vicious circle continues, with people wanting what they don't have and living on a fantasy island called "Someday I'll":

There is an island fantasy,
A "Someday I'll" we'll never see,
Where recession stops, inflation ceases,
Our mortgage is paid, our pay increases;
That "Someday I'll" where problems end,
Every piece of mail is from a friend;
Children are sweet and already grown,
And all the other nations can go it alone;
Where we all retire at forty-one
And play backgammon in the island sun;
Most unhappy people look to tomorrow
To ease the present day's hardship and sorrow.
They put happiness on layaway
And struggle through a blue Today.
But happiness cannot be sought.
It can't be earned; it can't be bought.
Life's most important revelation
Is the journey means more than the destination.
Happiness is where you are right now,
Pushing a pencil or pushing a plow,
Going to school or standing in line,

27

Watching and waiting or sipping the wine.
If you live in the past, you become senile.
If you live in the future, you're on "Someday I'll."
The fear of results is procrastination.
The joy of today is celebration.
You can save and slave, trudging mile after mile,
But you'll never set foot on "Someday I'll."
When you've paid your dues and put in your time,
Out of nowhere comes another mountain to climb.
From this day forward, make it your vow
To take "Someday I'll" and make it your Now!

Actions produce habits and habits produce accomplishments. Accomplishments determine your destiny. It all starts with action. If you take no action, there is nothing for God to bless.

Today is the tomorrow you talked about yesterday. You are exchanging one day of your life for it. When the sun sets, what will you have to show for it?

Procrastination

When we put off being happy until tomorrow, we are procrastinating. Procrastination masquerades as the solution to every problem. When used, however, it produces only grief and despair.

Procrastination wears a dozen masks. It pretends to be caution, reason, prudent planning or even "waiting on the Lord." Continuing to pray about a matter after God has given clear direction is at least a waste of time—and may even be an expression of rebellion.

The Bible says, "Do not boast about tomorrow, for you do not know what a day may bring forth" (Prov. 27:1). Paul instructs us to "make the most of every opportunity" (Col. 4:5).

Tomorrow Never Comes

As a pastor for many years, it has often been my duty to stand by the bedside of people who were dying. In those final moments of life, I have heard some of the sweetest expressions of love and devotion that could be uttered by human lips.

I have never heard anyone say, How I wish I had spent more time at the office. I have, however, heard many people say things like, I wish we had taken that vacation together, or, I wish we had taken time to smell the roses as we raced through life.

What happened? They kept putting off being happy until tomorrow. And tomorrow never came.

Worry Kills Happiness

Postponing happiness puts our focus on the future, which we can do nothing about. This inevitably leads to worry.

Have you ever noticed how worry always comes at a bad time? Just when we need a clear mind and steady nerves to make an important decision, here comes worry, gnawing at our peace like a five-pound rat.

Worry is like a rocking chair. It gives us something to do, but it doesn't get us anywhere. Worry never robs tomorrow of its sorrows. It only saps today of its strength.

Worry is a killer. It makes cowards out of aggressive men. It fills the face with wrinkles. It paralyzes the mind so it cannot produce the ''better idea'' needed to solve the problem at hand.

Worry robs the body of rest. It sends us to work shattered, shaky and on the jagged edge. It is the mother of heart disease, high blood pressure and ulcers. It's not what we're eating—it's what's eating us!

Don't Worry!

Worry is sin. We are commanded not to worry five times in just one chapter of Scripture: Matthew 6. Over and over, like the tolling of a bell in a country churchyard, ring out the words, "Take no thought...take no thought...take no thought."

God's own Son cups His hands to His mouth and shouts, "Don't worry!"

Don't worry about your finances. "My God will meet all your needs according to his glorious riches in Christ Jesus" (Phil. 4:19).

Don't worry about your weaknesses. "The Lord is the stronghold of my life" (Ps. 27:1). "The people that do know their God shall be strong, and do exploits" (Dan. 11:32, KJV).

Don't worry about your frustrations. "You will keep in perfect peace him whose mind is steadfast, because he trusts in you" (Is. 26:3).

Don't worry about your enemies. "The one who is in you is greater than the one who is in the world" (1 John 4:4).

To worry is to put your faith in fear. It is to trust in the unpleasant. It is to believe in defeat and despair. It is a stream of doubt that surges through the mind, drowning optimism, hope and faith.

Worry Is a Rat!

An aviator was making a round-the-world trip. On one leg of his journey he heard a noise in the plane—it sounded like the gnawing of a rat. He was two hours from the nearest landing field. Not knowing what delicate instruments might be destroyed by the rat's sharp teeth, he began to worry.

Then he remembered that a rat is not made for the heights. It is made to live in dark holes in the ground. He nosed the plane higher and higher until the gnawing stopped. Two hours later when he landed, there in the cockpit lay a dead rat.

Worry is a rat. It cannot live in ''the secret places of the Most High'' (Ps. 91:1). It cannot breathe in the atmosphere of confidence and faith. If your life has been thrown off course by worry, climb higher. Come into the presence of the living God. Feel His peace, His power, His love—and know that worry must die in His presence.

HAPPINESS IS NOT FOUND IN FREEDOM

God has dignified man by weaving into his nature the divine gift of freedom.

Freedom! The word falls upon the ear like soft rain on a hot summer day. It speaks of hopes, dreams and human dignity. It ought to be a deep well of lasting happiness. But instead it is often a source of turmoil, trials and tears.

When we see what man has done with his God-given freedom, we can only wonder why God didn't make us without it. He could have bound us to His sovereign will as a machine is bound to ours, and thereby relieved us of the risks and consequences of choice.

But for reasons of His own, God chose to place us in a rough and risky world with the awesome power to accept or reject His truth, to make or mar our destiny, to climb to the heights or sink to the depths.

Limited Liberty

There is no such thing as absolute freedom. The stars don't have it: They are bound by the laws of the unseen hand of the universe. The oceans don't have it: They are bound by shoreline that will not retreat. Man doesn't have it: He is hemmed in by other men and by the laws they make.

The story is told of a man who bought lumber to build

a tool shed on his lot. He was notified by a city official that the building code would not permit him to erect a wooden structure there.

"This is my lot. You can't tell me what to do on my property!" he protested.

In due time he gave in and changed to using brick. He was informed at city hall that before he could build anything he had to have a permit.

"A permit? I'm not going to buy a permit!" he fumed.

Thoroughly angered now, he drove off in a huff, ran a red light and was pulled over by a patrol car. He paid his fine, swearing that he would not live in a town that denied him his rights and his precious freedom.

He packed his belongings, loaded up his car and took off. When he reached the city limits he was halted by a health inspector: "You can't leave this town. It's been quarantined for smallpox."

You see? There simply is no such thing as absolute freedom.

Freedom From Responsibility?

To most young people, freedom means liberation from the restraints of their parents. They don't want to be hemmed in by stuffy moral standards. They don't want to be limited by curfews. They don't want to be shackled by responsibilities. They want the freedom of an adult and the responsibilities of a child.

This quest for freedom without responsibility is repeated millions of times every year by people of all ages. Husbands and fathers leave their wives and children for new lovers. Teenagers leave home, yelling over their shoulders at their weeping parents, "Don't try to tell me what to do!" They are free from all discipline, restraint and responsibility—or so they think.

Remember the prodigal son? God's watchdog, conscience,

barked at him every step of the way into the "far country" to which he journeyed. The rights he had demanded from his father didn't produce the happiness he was sure was out there waiting for him. The more he got what he wanted, the less he wanted what he got.

He left home saying, "Father, give me!" He came back with the stench of swine on him, saying, "Father, forgive me!" He discovered what every young person must learn: Freedom without responsibility is just another kind of tyranny.

Slaves to Our Own Choices

Aldous Huxley's story *Eyeless of Gaza* is about wealthy, educated people emancipated from all moral restraints. They are not happy. They are pathetically empty, with no capacity for loyalty or love toward anyone. They chatter endlessly about their right to be happy, their right to be free. In fact, they are enslaved by their choices.

The Bible teaches us that people who sin, who do not follow truth and righteousness, are always slaves. Only those who follow truth and right are truly free. Jesus lived under a vicious dictator—Herod—yet He was made free by the truth, while Herod lived in a marble penitentiary called a palace.

Freedom to Serve

God gives us freedom. Freedom for what? Freedom to do our own thing? Freedom to ignore the boundaries God has placed on everything and everyone in the universe?

No! God set us free from the law of sin and death so that we might serve one another in love. "Live as free men," Peter writes, "but do not use your freedom as a cover-up for evil; live as servants of God" (1 Pet. 2:16).

We are never truly free until we are voluntarily mastered by something greater than ourselves. We see this in the story of God's leading the children of Israel out of bondage in Egypt. They had been slaves; they were accustomed to being told what to do and when to do it. When God led them out of bondage, He did not say, "You're free to do as you like. Let's party!" He took them straight to Mt. Sinai and gave them the Ten Commandments.

When Jesus preached His first sermon, He said He had come to set the captives free. Yet the first step He made in the process was to bind them to Himself with the call, "Follow Me."

"Make Me Your Captive"

Bob Bartlett, the famous explorer, tells of a voyage on which his party brought back a number of exotic birds. One particular bird constantly clamored and clawed at his cage. About mid-ocean, it finally escaped. In utter ecstasy it flew away and disappeared in the pale blue sky. Bartlett and his team assumed the bird was lost forever.

But several hours later, to their surprise, they saw the bird coming back to the ship with drooping wings. Panting and breathless, the feathered prodigal flopped onto the deck. How desperately he had sought that ship again! It was no longer a prison that denied his freedom. It was a home, and the only way across the deep and endless sea.

There is no freedom until we are bound to something greater than ourselves. There is no liberty but the liberty to serve one another in the love of God. Every other "freedom" is an illusion. We batter and bruise ourselves in vain attempts to get away from God, only to discover that He is the only way across the deep and endless sea of life. Only when we are willing to say, "Make me Your captive, Lord," will we know true freedom. That's the day we will be happy in an unhappy world.

3

Happiness Is a Choice

I hate phones. I often tell my congregation that if I wake up in eternity and hear a telephone ringing, I'll know I've gone the wrong way. My secretary has a sign on her desk that reads, "This ministry is protected by an attack secretary!" She has the gift of shielding me from the distractions that come by way of AT&T's plastic monster.

But one Monday morning she burst into my office with a worried look on her face. "Pastor," she said, "this is one call you'd better take."

"You've Got to Help Me!"

Her quavering tone should have been warning enough. When I placed the receiver to my ear I heard the blood-curdling scream of a terrorized woman.

"Help me! Pastor, he's going to kill himself!"

"Who is? Who's going to kill himself?" I yelled back.

"My husband! Please! You've got to come right away!"

By now I recognized the voice. She was a gracious lady who had been to my office for counseling. She was married to a man who seemed to have everything: houses, lands, sports cars, condos, beautiful children and a lovely wife.

"He's in the bathroom with the door locked," she sobbed into the phone. "I just know he's committing suicide. Pastor, you've got to help me!"

I bolted from my office, slid behind the wheel of my station wagon and sped across San Antonio as though the interstate were the Indianapolis Motor Speedway. When I arrived at the house I could hear the tormented cries of the wife coming from inside.

She met me at the door. Her eyes were filled with horror and tears streaked her face.

"He's still in the bathroom," she cried. "Can you get him to come out?"

I went upstairs and tried the bathroom door. Locked. I was in no mood to administer the Harvard Temperament Test through a locked door, so I applied a technique more often employed by a blitzing middle linebacker. I lowered my shoulder and plowed into the door at full force. The door ripped off its hinges, taking the door frame and me along with it. I landed with a crash on the bathroom floor.

"Let Me Die, Pastor"

The husband lay on the floor, too, his face pale from loss

of blood. He had viciously slashed his right wrist with a straight razor. He lay there watching the rich, red arterial blood squirt onto the white marble floor with each beat of his heart. He was entirely serious about killing himself.

I knew he'd be dead in a matter of minutes without emergency medical treatment. I gripped his wrist to stop the flow of blood. He jerked it back from me, moaning, "Let me die, pastor. Let me die!"

"You *will* die if I don't get this bleeding stopped," I shouted at him.

"Good," he said. "I'm tired of living. I don't want to live anymore."

"When you wake up in hell you just might feel different about that," I snapped.

His wife and teenage children were in the hall, weeping hysterically. "Call the hospital and tell them we're on our way," I shouted.

I picked the man up and carried him down to the car. I threw him onto the back seat like a bale of hay, all the while clutching his slashed wrist. My suit was covered with blood.

"Where Did I Go Wrong?"

By now the man was quite weak—barely conscious, in fact. But he mustered enough strength to try to pull his hand away one more time. I decided I'd had enough wrestling. I closed my hand into a fist and landed a love-packed haymaker right on his chin. He collapsed like a dime-store accordion.

When we got to the hospital he was rushed to the emergency room, where he received a transfusion and had his veins sewn up by a gifted surgeon. When he finally regained consciousness and realized he was going to live—and have to face the harsh realities of life—he began to sob.

"Where did I go wrong?" he wept. "How did I get from where I was to where I am? Pastor, can you tell me how

I can get my life together and be happy again?''

Choosing Happiness

"Happiness begins with a choice," I told him. "You're in this hospital as a result of poor choices. You chose to break the laws of God and now you're suffering the consequences. You can be happy the day you choose to obey the divine principles of truth recorded in the Word of God."

The man had tried to kill himself, it came out, because his mistress was pregnant and was about to file a massive lawsuit exposing his private life. As a high-profile executive with a major company, the adverse publicity created by such a suit would doubtless cost him his high-paying job with all its prestige and perks. It would also cost him the respect of his children and his church and might very well cost him his marriage to a gracious but unsuspecting wife.

Counting the Cost

There's a high price to be paid for low living. When the husband sneaked off to meet his beautiful mistress at various posh hotels, it was exciting. When he locked the door and fell into a bed fragrant with her costly perfume, it was thrilling.

But when she became pregnant, it wasn't so much fun anymore. When she tried to make him live up to his pillow-talk promises, all the gusto was gone. When she went to the most powerful law firm in town and hired a squad of lawyers to eat him alive, it wasn't exciting at all. And when the lawsuit was filed, and he went home knowing he had to tell his wife and children before the ten o'clock news did, suicide seemed the only way out.

Had he counted the cost *before* adventuring with his enticing mistress, he would no doubt have made very different choices.

Happiness Never Just Happens

Many people think of happiness as something that just happens. If it happens to happen to them, terrific! If not, they curse their bad luck.

But happiness never just happens. It comes to us by our own choice. We decide whether to be happy or miserable, peaceful or anxious, fearful or serene. Much more of our lot in life than we realize proceeds from our choices.

"Now Choose Life"

Moses knew the power of choice to bring blessings or curses upon the nation of Israel. In one of history's most dramatic statements, he stood before all Israel and shouted with all the power of his aged voice:

> This day I call heaven and earth as witnesses against you that I have set before you life and death, blessings and curses. *Now choose life*, so that you and your children may live (Deut. 30:19, italics added).

When Abraham and Lot stood together on the fertile plains of Jordan, Lot made the choice that was to be his undoing. "So Lot chose for himself the whole plain of the Jordan" (Gen. 13:11). He pitched his tent toward Sodom, ignoring the moral and spiritual dangers.

Hear the hissing of the brimstone as it falls from the sky, bringing annihilation to Sodom. See the sons and daughters of Lot running in panic, futilely seeking a place of refuge. This was the consequence of their father's choice.

"Choose for Yourselves"

Joshua gathered the children of Israel together for his farewell address. He reviewed God's blessings upon Israel. He called upon Israel to abandon their idols and serve the true

God. He closed his address with one of the most memorable statements in history. *"Choose for yourselves* this day whom you will serve," he cried. Then he made clear what his choice would be: "...As for me and my household, we will serve the Lord" (Josh. 24:15, italics added).

When the apostle Paul was on the road to Damascus, God knocked him to his knees and struck him blind. Paul had a choice to make. He could remain blind for life or he could obey God. The Acts of the Apostles records Paul's choice. He didn't ask, Why me? or even say, Poor me. He obeyed. He picked himself up from the dust of the Damascus road, set his face like flint and shook Rome to its roots with the power of the gospel of Christ.

For or Against Jesus Christ

When Jesus stood before Pilate on trial for his life, Pilate said, "What shall I do, then, with Jesus who is called Christ?" (Matt. 27:22). That is the choice every man or woman on earth must make: either for Christ or against Him.

Jesus Christ is not just a good man or a great moral teacher. He is either Lord, liar or lunatic. He is either God's sinless Son or He is the greatest charlatan who ever lived. If He is the Lord, we must serve Him with all our hearts, minds, souls and strength. If not, we must ignore Him. We must ignore His teachings, His death and resurrection, His promises to return with power and great glory.

The choice we make about Jesus Christ, above all others, determines the happiness quotient of our lives. It is impossible to do nothing about Jesus Christ. Not to decide for Him is to decide against Him. There is no such thing as indecision. Until this choice is made, we can never be happy in an unhappy world.

Who'd Choose Unhappiness?

Abraham Lincoln said, "Most people are about as happy as they choose to be" (from *Light From Many Lamps* by Lillian E. Watson, Simon and Schuster). How true! It's hard to imagine that someone might actually choose unhappiness over happiness. But millions do every day, often for reasons even they don't fully understand. Some choose unhappiness to manipulate those around them, to get attention or sympathy. Some choose unhappiness indirectly, because they don't know where or how to find happiness. Some religious people choose unhappiness as living proof of their "superior spirituality."

A minister was preaching on happiness. His congregation was laughing with joy. Suddenly a self-righteous religious peacock stood and icily rebuked the minister and the congregation for their laughter. Without missing a beat, the minister intoned, "Let us now allow this unhappy brother to lead us in a moment of corporate misery."

The Last Freedom

Fritz Kunkle said that our last freedom in life is to determine our attitude in any given situation.

We usually have no control over what happens to us. But we are responsible for how we respond to what happens to us. The Bible has a lot to say about choosing our attitudes:

- "As he thinketh in his heart, so is he" (Prov. 23:7, KJV).
- "Everything is possible for him who believes" (Mark 9:23).
- "I do believe; help me overcome my unbelief!" (Mark 9:24).
- "According to your faith will it be done to you" (Matt. 9:29)
- "Whatever is true, whatever is noble, whatever is right,

whatever is pure, whatever is lovely, whatever is admirable—
if anything is excellent or praiseworthy—think about such
things" (Phil. 4:8).

Setting the Tone

There are only two kinds of attitudes: good ones and bad
ones. Profound, eh? So is a marvelous poem my mother
taught me when I was a child. I've never forgotten it. It goes
like this:

> Two men looked out prison bars:
> One saw mud, the other stars.

Two men in exactly the same circumstance made opposite
choices that determined their capacity to be happy. Which
choice would you have made?

Why not choose a positive attitude first thing in the morning, before things even have a chance to go wrong? King
David said, "This is the day the Lord has made; let us rejoice and be glad in it" (Ps. 118:24). Paul wrote, "Rejoice
in the Lord always. I will say it again: Rejoice!" (Phil. 4:4).
That choice, when you get up in the morning, will set the
mood for your whole day.

Paul and Thomas

A positive attitude produces a good result; a negative
attitude produces a bad result. Compare the lives of the
apostles Paul and Thomas. Paul said, "I can do everything
through him who gives me strength" (Phil. 4:13). He was
three times given the notorious thirty-nine lashes. He was
shipwrecked, stoned and left for dead, the object of death
threats and public hatred. Yet he was able to write, "We
are hard pressed on every side, but not crushed; perplexed,
but not in despair; persecuted, but not abandoned; struck

down, but not destroyed'' (2 Cor. 4:8-9). He wrote that, as he wrote most of the New Testament, from a dark, damp, disease-infested jail cell. That's a positive result in an impossible situation.

Thomas had the benefit of three and a half years of following Christ and personally witnessing miracles that stagger the mind. Yet when Jesus rose from the dead and the other disciples ran to him with the news, Thomas just rolled out his lower lip and pouted, ''Unless I see the nail marks in his hands and put my finger where the nails were, and put my hand into his side, I will not believe it'' (John 20:25).

Two men, two different choices. One is forever branded as Doubting Thomas. The other is mentioned in hushed tones as the apostle of power who established the church of Jesus Christ.

"I Know I'm Dying"

Our attitudes don't have to be determined by our circumstances. I once stood by the bedside of a beautiful and courageous seventeen-year-old girl who was dying of cancer. I can stand by the deathbed of an adult who has lived a full, rich life and accept that all good things must end. But when I stand beside a dying child, I have to fight tears.

Rosie read my thoughts perfectly. Clutching her white Bible in her frail hands, she looked me straight in the eye and said, "Pastor, I know I'm dying. But isn't this a beautiful day? Every day is a gift from God." I felt ashamed of the petty circumstances I so often let control my attitude toward life. This teenage champion of courage didn't let the worst of circumstances control her attitude.

Who's in Control?

Circumstances control you only if you let them. Jesus said,

"Peace I leave with you; my peace I give you" (John 14:27). He did not utter these words from an ivory tower in some Shangri-la. He said it to His disciples the night before He was to be crucified by the Romans. He refused to let the circumstances control His attitude.

When Paul and Silas were in prison at Philippi, they sang at midnight. When the circumstances were at their worst, they were at their best. What did God do in response? He sent a squadron of angels who shook the jail off its foundations with an earthquake. Paul walked out of there with the jailhouse keys in one hand and a new convert in the other—because he refused to be mastered by his circumstances.

Make Your Problems Disappear

Most people wait for their circumstances to change before they're willing to change their attitudes. The husband says, "I'll change when my wife changes." The wife says, "I'll change my attitude when my husband changes his." Standoff! Besides, they haven't learned that trying to change another person is as futile as trying to blow out a light bulb.

We change husbands, wives, colleges, churches, business ventures and professional goals before we are willing to change our attitudes. If we will exercise man's final freedom, the freedom to determine what our attitudes will be in any given situation, many of our problems will simply vanish.

Making Friends or Enemies?

Our attitudes toward others determine their attitudes toward us. If we adopt a negative, fault-finding attitude, of course no one wants to be around us.

A doctor told his patient, "Ma'am, the dog that bit you had rabies, and I'm afraid you've waited too long for rabies shots to be of any help. It's time for you to make out a will."

"May I borrow a pen and some paper?" asked the woman calmly. She began writing—and didn't stop for over an hour.

"That's the longest will I've ever seen," the doctor said.

"It's not a will," the woman replied. "It's a list of all the people I'm going to bite when I get out of here."

Some people make others happy when they arrive. Others make them happy when they leave. Which are you?

Miracles Come in Cans

Our attitudes determine our attainments. A supermarket is a building filled with cans. Wouldn't it be wonderful if we could buy a sixteen-ounce can of peace? or love? or happiness? Well, we can. Miracles come in cans. They begin when we say, "I can."

I can climb this mountain and whip the giant at the top. I can lose weight. I can be a better marriage partner. I can quit smoking. I can live beyond my limitations. I can— because "everything is possible for him who believes" (Mark 9:23).

• Stop saying, "I haven't got it." You do have it. You're just afraid to use it.

• Stop saying, "I'm a loser." You're not a loser. You're a winner with a sorry attitude.

• Stop saying, "I'm not educated enough." So what? I've graduated from three universities, and I can tell you that some of the dumbest people on earth are hiding out there.

• Stop saying, "I don't know the right people." Do you know God? He's rather influential on this planet!

• Stop saying, "I'm handicapped." Helen Keller was blind, deaf and dumb. Yet she graduated from college with honors.

• Stop saying, "I've tried and failed." Moses tried to deliver the Hebrews from the iron grip of Egypt's bondage. He failed and fled to the backside of the wilderness for forty years. Then God called him to return to the scene of his failure and command Pharaoh to let His people go. Ten plagues later, Moses led his brethren out of the chains of slavery into the milk and honey of the land of promise. He tried. He failed. But he was willing to try again.

Staying Afloat

Ever feel like giving up on life? on your marriage? on your professional goals? Let me share with you one of my favorite poems by Pameii, called "Made of the Right Stuff":

A little brown cork
Fell in the path of a whale
Who lashed it down
With his angry tail.
But in spite of its blows
It quickly arose
And floated serenely
Before his nose.
Said the cork to the whale,
"You may sputter and frown
But you never, never can keep me down,
For I'm made of the stuff
That is buoyant enough
To float instead of to drown."

Are We Willing to Be Happy?

Our attitudes don't have to be permanent. We can change our attitudes, just as soon as we're willing to. Our attitudes will determine the quality of relationships we will have with our wives, our husbands, our children, our bosses—even God Himself. Our choice of attitude controls the quality of our happiness for today, and today is the only unit of time we really have.

Yesterday is gone. Tomorrow may never come. We can

only be happy today. And we can be just as happy as we decide to be.

Faith: Take It or Leave It?

Many people in today's world claim that faith is a "take it or leave it" item, one that makes little or no difference in the quality of life. Is this true?

Let's ask ourselves: What happens when a man loses faith in himself? or in God? or in the future? Does he sing for joy? Does he throw his arms around his companions with laughter, saying, "I have no faith in myself!" Is his face radiant with the glow of happiness?

Of course not. There is no joy. No peace. No happiness. Instead, trembling hands reach for mind-numbing tranquilizers, or for a drink to drown the sorrow, or for a snort of cocaine.

What happens when a woman loses faith in her marriage? Does she laugh for joy as she phones her lawyer? Does she call her friends together and celebrate the collapse of her life?

No. There are tears and agony of heart, expressing the pain of broken faith. Without faith in your marriage partner, home becomes hell on earth.

Do We Believe Too Much?

We sometimes get deceived because we believe too much. But it's more often true that we get cheated because we believe too little. The question must be asked: What can be accomplished without faith? The answer: Absolutely nothing.

The farmer plants his seed by faith that God will send the rain to make it grow. Everyone who eats is enjoying the fruit of living faith.

The physician makes his incision by faith that God can heal the patient.

We buy insurance policies on faith, trusting that the company will pay off when we have a claim.

That's Faith!

Noah built an ark without even having seen the first drop of rain, because faith is being "certain of what we do not see" (Heb. 11:1). Faith doesn't demand miracles; faith produces miracles. Imagine getting on a boat you built with your bare hands, filling it with tigers, lions and snakes, and taking a forty-day cruise with your wife and family. That's faith!

Abraham, at age one hundred, went to his ninety-year-old wife, Sarah, and said, "Turn off the television, honey. God told me we're going to have a baby." That's faith! Later Abraham offered his son Isaac as a living sacrifice to the Lord, believing God would raise him from the dead. And God provided another sacrifice. That's faith!

Faith is the soul daring to go further than the natural eye can see. Faith is a choice, not an argument. A decision, not a debate. A commitment, not a controversy.

Faith gives us the power to walk fearlessly, run confidently and live victoriously. No one need live in doubt when he can pray in faith. Even if our faith cannot yet move mountains, it can give us the power to climb over them.

Faith Is All We Need

A skeptic once said to me, "Preacher, all you Christians have going for you is faith."

I replied, "You're right! And that's all we need!"

The Bible says:

• Our faith is the victory that overcomes the world (1 John 5:4).

• "Without faith it is impossible to please God" (Heb. 11:6).

• "Everything is possible for him who believes" (Mark 9:23).

Is faith important for living happy in an unhappy world? Just try living one day without it!

Imagine, for example, that everyone you know is lying to you or about you. See that couple chatting quietly in the corner? Tell yourself they're talking about you. When you deposit your paycheck, make yourself believe the bank is stealing your money and you'll never see it again. When you're passed up for a promotion at work, tell yourself there's a conspiracy in the front office to hold you back. When your doctor tells you that you need an emergency operation to save your life, persuade yourself that he's lying. He only wants to operate because he's after the insurance money.

You see? Try living one day without faith and you're on your way to the nut house. Faith is the fabric that clothes the heart, soul, mind and body with old-fashioned, overflowing, heaven-sent happiness.

Happiness and Holiness

What about holiness? What does it have to do with happiness?

The traditional meaning of the word "holy" is "to be set apart for God." Too many churches, in the name of holiness, have majored on the negative and overlooked Paul's teaching that the "don't go there, don't do that" approach to religion has nothing to do with either holiness or happiness (see Col. 2:20-23).

I was raised in a church where the eleventh commandment was, "If it's fun, it's sin." I was sixteen before I could muster up the courage to see my first movie. There I sat, watching Cecil B. DeMille's magnificent presentation of *The Ten Commandments*, terrified I would get caught or drop dead and wake up in the flames of hell—all for watching

Moses cross the Red Sea.

"You can tell where the devil lives in our town," we'd say in church. "You can see his forked tail sticking up out of the roof." We were referring to the television antennas. There was, of course, no television in our house. We weren't about to let Hopalong Cassidy corrupt us.

Dancing, right up there with murder and adultery—absolutely unthinkable. No cards, dominoes or dice were permitted in our home. Even the game Monopoly was forbidden because you had to roll those dice to play it. (I later learned to play all these games—in seminary. But I still can't dance a step to save my life.)

Holiness: From the Inside Out

Holiness is inward likeness to God. It's being like God from the inside out. The Bible speaks of our "participating in the divine nature" (2 Pet. 1:4). Holiness is reflected in our outward actions. But it's not determined by our outward actions.

Our faith is a holy faith. Our book is the holy Bible. Our God is the holy God who sits upon the throne of His holiness. Our Savior is the holy child Jesus. Our city is the holy city, the New Jerusalem, coming down out of heaven from God. Our Spirit is the Holy Spirit. Our song is sung by the holy angels surrounding the throne of God: "Holy, holy, holy is the Lord." The Bible records the command of God: "Be holy, because I am holy" (1 Pet. 1:16).

Is anyone interested in holiness? Our society seems to feel that a little dirt is necessary for the development of the instinctual man.

Well, dirt in the yard helps the grass grow, and dirt in the garden helps the flowers grow. But dirt piled in the living room is out of place. And dirt piled in our thoughts produces sin, whose end products are guilt, pain and suffering. If you want to be happy, be holy.

Imitating Jesus

But how? How do we become holy? It's simple. Imitate Jesus. He's the pattern. Speak as He spoke. Think as He thought. Act as He acted. Love as He loved.

We shrink back from the word "holiness" because we're so intimidated by the concept. "Me? Holy? Get serious!" But if holiness were not possible, God would not ask it of us.

Holiness is both positional and progressive. When we come to the Lord and ask Him to forgive our sins through the blood of His cross, that's positional holiness. We receive it at the cross. We don't earn it. We accept it by faith.

Progressive holiness is that which is worked out in us over the years. It is our being natural and letting God be supernatural. It is not using religious cliches or long, flowery prayers. It is allowing God's love to live in us and through us—so naturally that people are attracted to the inner glow of divine happiness.

Attitude Over Circumstances

Happiness is found in holiness. Happiness is not haphazard; it's a choice of attitude over circumstance.

Let's explore together the secret of the eight principles of happiness established in the Sermon on the Mount. They are commonly known as the beatitudes. They are God's blueprint for happiness. These statements constitute the Magna Carta of Happiness. They are our foundation for being happy in an unhappy world.

4

Happiness Comes
Through Poverty

Happy are the poor in spirit,
for theirs is the kingdom of heaven.

Join me, in the theater of your mind, on the shore of the
Sea of Galilee. We are part of a curious and anxious throng
that has gathered from Jerusalem, Judea and beyond the Jordan to hear the controversial rabbi, Jesus of Nazareth.

It's a hot, humid day. A soft wind blows across the placid
waters of the ancient sea. We hear loud voices expressing
divergent opinions about Jesus.

"How can we be happy when Rome has robbed us of our
freedoms?" says one man. "While we're being taxed into
poverty, this Jesus has actually accepted a tax collector as
one of His followers."

"Perhaps He is the promised Messiah who will lead us

to crush the Roman oppressors!'' cries another.

''Get serious,'' says his friend. ''How can a handful of Jewish farmers whip these cold-blooded killers? We'll all die in slavery and poverty. You might as well get used to the idea.''

The Magna Carta of Happiness

Suddenly a man appears, with twelve followers, walking down the narrow path leading from Capernaum. Word ripples through the crowd: ''He's coming!'' The twelve men search for a comfortable place for the rabbi to sit while He teaches principles of truth that will guide the eternal souls of men forever.

It is a moment history will never forget. The crowd hushes. Jesus sits on a flat rock at the base of the grassy slope, allowing the gentle breeze to carry His words clearly and swiftly to the ears of His eager listeners.

He opens His mouth and begins to speak. ''Happy are those....'' He gives eight principles of happiness. They are simple principles. But they are profound enough that the world still has not fully comprehended them after two thousand years. Eight statements that constitute the Magna Carta of Happiness. Eight statements that represent the divine blueprint for being happy in an unhappy world.

Jesus Is in the Happiness Business

When He was born, the angels over Bethlehem announced "good news of great joy that will be for all the people" (Luke 2:10). He ordained happiness by attending the wedding at Cana. The theme of His first sermon was happiness. The closing picture of Him, in the book of Revelation, portrays Him as a bridegroom coming to claim His bride. The wedding reception lasts for seven years in the joyous splendor of heaven.

Take a look at the average church congregation on any given Sunday morning. They look like advance agents for a cyclone. Their faces are as droopy as saxophones. They look like Bible-carrying bulldogs baptized in lemon juice!

They go to work on Monday morning saved, sour, sanctified and petrified. They look at their co-workers and say, "Don't you want to know Jesus? Look what He's done for me!"

Don't be fooled: Christianity certainly involves hardship and discipline. But it is founded on the solid rock of old-fashioned happiness. Jesus is in the happiness business. If we lose our joy, we've lost our credibility in this unhappy world.

Absolute Commitment

Happiness begins with an absolute commitment to Christ. There are two groups of people who have come to hear this sermon about happiness: the disciples, who have made an absolute commitment to follow Jesus, and the multitudes, a curious mob committed to nothing.

A disciple is someone who has forsaken all to follow Christ. Jesus established the entrance requirements early on when He said, "Anyone who loves his father or mother more than me is not worthy of me; anyone who loves his son or daughter more than me is not worthy of me; and anyone who does not take his cross and follow me is not worthy of me. Whoever finds his life will lose it, and whoever loses his life for my sake will find it" (Matt. 10:37-39). Jesus does not call us to a life of convenience. He calls us to a life of commitment.

Jesus: Straight Shooter

Happy are the poor in spirit. How different from the attitude of the Christians in Laodicea, who said, "I am rich;

55

I have acquired wealth and do not need a thing" (Rev. 3:17).

How many Christians today share their point of view! So much of the church is saturated with the Dr. Feelgood theology. If it feels good, do it, and when it gets hard, get out.

That is not the message of Christ. Everywhere He went there were conflict, controversy and conversion. He was crucified as an insurrectionist considered too dangerous to live. He was not "gentle Jesus, meek and mild." He was a straight shooter.

Four Religious Responses

Four major religious groups were represented among the multitude that listened to Jesus' sermon: the Pharisees, the Sadducees, the Essenes and the Zealots.

The Pharisees. When Jesus said, "Happy are the poor in spirit," I believe He was looking right at the Pharisees, piercing their proud hearts. The Pharisees believed that happiness was found in legalism. They were forerunners of the "we don't smoke, we don't chew, and we don't run with those who do" crowd.

The Sadducees. This group believed that happiness was found in modernism and liberalism. "Ours is an up-to-date religion," they would say, "full of the latest philosophy. There's no cross to bear. There are no conflicts because there is no confrontation. The Scripture? A delightful, romantic allegory. Sin? What on earth is that?"

The Essenes. They believed that happiness was found in isolation from the world. Isolation is a state of being cut off from other people. Its opposite is absorption: the state of being so saturated with others that you forget who you are. Your own identity is lost and your goals blurred on the treadmill of trying to please others.

Happiness can never be found in absolute isolation or in absolute absorption. It lies somewhere in between. It is not found living alone in the desert as the Essenes believed. Happiness is knowing who we are and to whom we belong.

The Zealots. These hotheads thought happiness lay in political revolution. "Let's run the Romans out of town," they said, "and then we can all be happy."

Today many Christians are crying, "Let's take charge of the government! Then we can be happy." But in view of recent scandals that have shaken the church to its roots, it would appear that we need to take charge of ourselves first. Before praying for power to take over the government, let's pray for power to develop an ear sensitive to the voice of the Holy Spirit and a tender heart toward God and man.

The Contradiction

Happiness is not the product of external conditions. We've got it backward. Happiness doesn't depend on the kind of house a man lives in; it depends on the kind of man who lives in the house. Happiness doesn't depend on the dress the lady wears; it depends on the lady who wears the dress. Our society says:

"Happy is the man who makes a million dollars!"

"Happy is the woman who marries a man who makes a million dollars!"

"Happy is the go-getter, the guy who gets what he wants, when he wants it and just the way he likes it."

"Happiness is doing your own thing."

"Happiness is going for the gusto."

"Happiness is being rich, powerful and famous."

Jesus, the architect of the human soul, cups His hands to His mouth and cries out, "Wrong! Happy are the poor in spirit." What a contradiction! How far removed from the carnal mind of this pleasure-seeking generation!

Broken in Spirit

What does "poor in spirit" mean? It does not mean being a trembly lipped religious doormat. It does not mean being a pious introvert trying to blend into the wallpaper. It does not mean being someone with no self-esteem who crawls, cringes and grovels through life.

It does mean happy are the broken in spirit. Happy are those people who allow the hand of God to crush their carnal nature so that they are no longer conformed to this world but are transformed into the glorious image of Christ. Happy are those who allow the hand of the Master to remove their imperfections, remaking them into a vessel of honor pleasing to their Maker.

Before the power of the atom could be unleashed, science had to devise a way to "smash" it. The secret of its power lay in its being crushed. Before a grape can be made into fine wine, it must be crushed. On the vine, it's a thing of beauty. But after it's crushed, it's a thing of blessing.

Jesus lists being broken in spirit as the number one priority in the pursuit of happiness. Only when the carnal nature is crushed and the inner poison removed can there be complete healing and a new beginning. Anything else is just new patches sewn over old cloth. It's new wine in old bottles. It's a futile religious charade that guarantees nothing but everlasting frustration.

Happiness and Humility

Happiness never comes to the proud. The Bible tells us that God opposes the proud (James 4:6) and that haughty eyes are detestable to Him (Prov. 6:16-17).

In the first chapter of his letter to the Romans, Paul lists some of the most despicable people on the face of the earth. Among them are those "filled with every kind of wickedness, evil, greed and depravity," those "full of envy, murder, strife, deceit and malice," and those he calls the "arrogant and boastful" (Rom. 1:29-30). In other words, the proud.

Being broken in spirit was utter rubbish to the Romans. They worshipped the god of power. "If you want to be happy," the Romans said, "knock your enemy to the ground, put a sword to his throat and say, 'Make a wish!' "

To the equally proud Jews, being poor in spirit was the last thing in the world to do to be happy. They had their own formula for happiness, and poverty of spirit was definitely not one of the ingredients.

Discerning the Difference

How are we to identify those who are broken in spirit and those who are diseased with pride? Three illustrations in the Bible nail it down for us.

The first is Jesus' story of the Pharisee and the tax collector. These two men went to the temple to pray. The Pharisee prayed, "God, I thank You that I am not like other men— robbers, evildoers, adulterers—or even like this tax collector." The tax collector, standing at a distance, "would not even look up to heaven, but beat his breast and said, 'God, have mercy on me, a sinner' " (Luke 18:11-13).

The Prodigal's Brother

The second illustration is found in the parable of the prodigal son and his older brother (Luke 15:11-32). The prodigal went into the far country and broke all the rules. He lost his good name, his father's fortune and all his worthless friends. He found himself living in a pigsty. Then, the Bible says, he "came to his senses" and said, "I will go back to my father and say to him, 'Father, I have sinned.' "

And he did. He shook off the slime and began the long

journey home, rehearsing his speech of repentance. His father saw him coming from a long distance and ran to him and embraced him. There were tears of reunion and restoration.

A family fiesta was planned to celebrate the return of a son who had been considered as good as dead. Everyone was happy—except for the prodigal's older brother. This proud, religious sourpuss was angry.

He whined, "Father, I've stayed home like a good boy and kept all the rules. When did you ever give me a party? Now that this son of yours (not "my brother" but "this son of yours") has come home bankrupt after living with harlots, you reward him with a celebration!" The rancor in his voice reflected the rot in his soul.

The Power to Stoop Low

The third illustration is the account of Jesus the night before His crucifixion. The disciples had been jockeying for position in the new kingdom. The mother of James and John had been putting on a full-court press to get her boys in top positions of the administration.

It came time to wash their dirty feet. The only one who had the power to stoop low and take on the menial task was the Son of God. Why? Because He was the only one in the room not bound by pride. He was the only one with a servant's heart. The others were career-minded and ego-centered and proud. In time, God put each and every one of them through His crusher until they came out as servants. But they had to be broken to be usable. And so do we.

"Good Thinking, Jonah!"

God doesn't force us to change our minds about our pride. But He does give us ample opportunity to re-evaluate our position. Jonah found himself in the belly of a great fish when

God whispered in his ear, "Jonah, if you'll do what I called you to do, I'll program this fish to deposit you on the beach. Otherwise, this fish just had lunch. What'll it be?"

Jonah screamed, "I'll obey! I'll obey! Forgive me for being so stubborn and full of pride."

God said, "Good thinking, Jonah!"

Jonah waded to shore, slimy, smelly seaweed around his neck, bloodshot eyes, trembling with fear, his pride finally crushed, crying out to the Ninevites as God had commanded him, "Repent!"

Saul of Tarsus was knocked to the ground and struck blind on the road to Damascus. God whispered in his ear, "Saul, you can quit persecuting Me and these new Christians, or you can stay blind. What's your pleasure?"

Saul replied, "What do You want me to do? Just name it!"

And God said, "Attaboy, Saul!"

God plays hardball. When He spots pride in your life He goes after it the way a surgeon goes after cancer. He'll put you flat on your back in a full body cast for a moment of reflection. He'll take the possessions that are the basis of your mentality and scatter them to the four winds. He'll make your bed like coals of fire in the night. You'll never know rest until you make your peace with God.

The First Step

Only when we are crushed and remolded in the hands of the master potter can we enter the kingdom of God. Jesus picked up a little child and addressed His hardened adult audience: "Unless you change and become like little children, you will never enter the kingdom of heaven. Therefore, whoever humbles himself like this child is the greatest in the kingdom of heaven" (Matt. 18:3-4).

Millions of America's tormented legions flood through the doors of our churches every Sunday proud, religious, unteachable, cold, jaded, resentful, hurting and hateful—about as unlike a humble little child as can be. We are searching for happiness. But we can find it only when we allow the loving hand of God to break us and remake us into vessels that please Him. This is the first step toward true happiness. Why not take it right now?

5

Happiness Comes Through Mourning

Happy are those who mourn,
for they shall be comforted.

"**D**id you hear what the rabbi said?" a man in the crowd scoffed to his companion. " 'Happy are those who mourn.' If happiness and mourning go together, then we Jews must be in heaven!"

Do happiness and mourning go together? What a paradox! How flatly it contradicts today's hedonistic world view! How can crying and joy go together? How can the perfume of happiness be extracted from the gall of sorrow?

Who in his natural mind would think of congratulating a person whose face was wet with tears? "It's nice to see you crying today, Mary. Keep it up, love. It's good for you."

Good Company

When we weep, we're in good company. When Lazarus died, Jesus wept. When He knelt on the Mount of Olives and looked out over the city of Jerusalem, He wept. When Paul left the town of Ephesus, he and the elders wept with sorrow at their parting. John wept on the isle of Patmos because no one was found worthy to open the scroll that would reveal God's plans.

But Jesus is not saying, "Happy are the crybabies, for they shall get what they want. Happy are those dedicated to feeling guilty even when they haven't done anything wrong. Happy are those who have learned to whine their way to maximum attention. Happy are those who love root canals and IRS audits." He says, "Happy are those who mourn, *for they shall be comforted.*"

The God of All Comfort

Do you understand the implications of this? The God of all comfort promises to comfort us.

• The God who comforted Abraham as he walked toward Mt. Moriah to sacrifice his beloved Isaac—that God will comfort us!

• The God who comforted Paul on the raging sea moments before he was shipwrecked—that God will comfort us!

• The God who comforted the fathers of the church as they were being burned alive by their persecutors—that God will comfort us!

The first thing we'll feel in eternity is the gentle hand of God, wiping the tears from our eyes. Even now, in the dark of night when our hearts are breaking, He sits beside us. When we've been abandoned by our dearest friend on earth and feel so absolutely alone, He picks us up in His massive arms and holds us close until the storm passes by.

Shout it from the housetops to the unhappy legions of earth: "We shall be comforted!" Who says so? The God of all comfort says so.

Mourning Is Healthy

Have you ever heard the expression "good grief"? It's true. Grief is healthy. A tear in the eye tells of at least one spring in the soul. It may lie buried beneath emotional scars, a bitter divorce, rejection by parents, a litany of bitter memories that will not die. But that one little tear trickling down our cheeks cries out, "I'm alive!"

Every Sunday morning at Cornerstone Church, immediately after the sermon, I invite all who wish to respond to the gospel to come forward to the altar. When I was a child, we used to call it "the mourner's bench." People come forward with tears streaming down their faces.

Why? Because the Lord is at work. Shattered dreams are being rebuilt, fractured marriages restored, ruptured relationships healed by the power of God. The pressures of life are easing and the burden of sin lifting as people bask in the happiness that only God can give. They look sad on the outside, but they're happy on the inside.

God's Therapy

Tears are living proof of life. The man who cannot shed tears is not fully alive.

One day a woman called my office asking if I would talk to her husband, who was manifesting signs of severe depression. Their eighteen-year-old son had been killed two months before in a blazing auto accident, and the father's heart was broken. His torture was compounded because he embraced the mentality that it isn't manly to cry.

When I arrived at the home, I found the man in the back

yard, pacing back and forth like a caged lion. We chatted a few moments as I searched for a tactful way to broach the painful subject of his son's tragic death.

Suddenly he blurted out, "Tears are for the weak, preacher. I'm too hard and cold to cry. I'm like steel inside."

"That's a pity," I said. "And dangerous, too."

"Why?" he asked.

"Because the only thing steel can do under stress is snap and break," I said. "You may consider tears a sign of weakness, but they are really God's therapy for a broken heart. On the other side of tears is God's peace. Don't be afraid to cry."

He brushed off my advice. Two days later he put a .357 Magnum in his mouth and blew the top of his head off. He couldn't bend like a supple tree planted beside rivers of living water. He could only snap under the pressure.

Happy are those who mourn, who can weep like a child, sob it out in their private Gethsemane and later find relief in the rich laughter of heavenly consolation. They shall be comforted indeed.

Mourning Over Wrongdoing

One night my ten-year-old son called me to his room. It was almost 10:30—two hours past his bedtime. As I walked up the winding stairs, I could hear him crying softly in the darkness. When I opened the door, I could see moonlight reflected from cheeks wet with tears.

"What's the matter, Matthew?" I asked quietly.

"Today I said some things that offended the Lord," he said. "Would you pray with me that God would forgive me for what I said?"

I didn't ask what it was he'd said. Even if it was horrible, God would forgive it. And even if it was trivial, it was still serious to Matthew. I knelt beside his bed and we prayed together until he felt comforted.

As I walked back to my bedroom I prayed, "Lord, don't let me lose the heart of a child. Don't let me get so cold and calloused that I forget how to mourn over things that offend You."

The Sting of Conscience

Paul speaks of people who have "lost all sensitivity" (Eph. 4:19). They are past feeling. Their consciences no longer sting when they break the law of God. It's a dangerous position to be in. Our consciences are supposed to hurt when we sin. It's how God alerts us to the need for repentance.

Socrates described conscience as the spouse from whom there is no divorce. Maybe we can't divorce our consciences, but we can stifle them until their voices are silent. Then we have, in Paul's words, "lost all sensitivity."

Remember Father Damien, the leper priest? In answer to God's call, he became a missionary to the lepers on the island of Molokai. For thirteen years he lived among them as their teacher, their companion and their friend.

At last the dread disease laid hold of him. One morning he spilled some boiling water on his foot and felt not the slightest hint of pain. Then he knew—he was doomed. The loss of feeling was proof that leprosy had conquered.

It is the same with us. When we become unable to mourn over our sin, when our consciences have been so seared that they no longer react to sin, we are morally doomed.

What about you? When you sin, does your conscience trouble you? Then be glad! Happy are those who mourn over wrongdoing, for they are truly alive.

Forgiveness Leads to Happiness

And that's not all. Happy are those who mourn over

wrongdoing, for they are being forgiven. And forgiveness leads to happiness.

Sin and happiness are never found together. Consider the lives of King Saul and King David.

Saul was handsome, powerful, the choice of the people. As long as the adulation of Israel was directed toward him, all was well.

Then came David's stunning victory over Goliath. When the army was returning from the field of battle, the women came out from all the towns of Israel to meet them. They danced and sang, "Saul has slain his thousands, and David his tens of thousands" (1 Sam. 18:7).

Saul Conquers His Conscience

Saul was enraged. He sent David away and then hunted him across the hills of Israel like an angry hound pursuing a fox. Slowly but surely Saul conquered his conscience. In earlier days he expelled witches and mediums from Israel. Now, having "lost all sensitivity," he disguised himself and went by night to the witch of Endor, grievously violating the law of God.

In all the Scriptures there is not the slightest hint that Saul ever mourned over his sin toward David, or over his defiance of God's law concerning witchcraft. He died in bitterness and anguish, utterly bereft of the joy that could have been his as God's anointed.

The Sin of David

Now consider King David. After many years on the throne, he became addicted to the nectar of power. When he saw the beautiful woman Bathsheba, he used his absolute authority to have her brought to him. He committed adultery with her and, to cover up his crime, craftily arranged for her husband to be killed.

God sent the prophet Nathan to King David. He told the king a story of a wealthy man who had stolen and eaten the only sheep of a poor man. David was enraged. "As surely as the Lord lives," he said, "the man who did this deserves to die!" Only then did Nathan point his finger at David and intone, "You are the man!"

At that moment, David's life before God hung in the balance. What decision would he make? Would he mourn for his sin? Or would he, like Saul, choose to override his conscience and ignore that voice of God? The Scriptures record his decision: "Then David said to Nathan, 'I have sinned against the Lord' " (2 Sam. 12:13).

Delivered From Spiritual Leprosy

That one simple statement delivered David from spiritual leprosy. He mourned his sin before God with tears. Listen to the shepherd king of Israel as he weeps before the Lord. Hear the mourning in his voice. Hear him moving from sadness to joy as he contemplates God's forgiveness in Psalm 51:1-2,7-8,12:

> Have mercy on me, O God,
>   according to your unfailing love;
> according to your great compassion
>   blot out my transgressions.
> Wash away all my iniquity
>   and cleanse me from my sin....
> Cleanse me with hyssop, and I will be clean;
>   wash me, and I will be whiter than snow.
> Let me hear joy and gladness;
>   let the bones you have crushed rejoice....
> Restore to me the joy of your salvation
>   and grant me a willing spirit, to sustain me.

Have you violated your conscience for the sake of carnal convenience? Are you approaching the precipice of "losing all sensitivity"? Being happy in an unhappy world requires mourning over wrongdoing so that we may know the joy of forgiveness.

Where Is God When It Hurts?

As a pastor, I know there are times when no words in human speech can remove the pain from the brokenhearted. Many of those times occur when a tragedy has befallen someone for no apparent reason. A child dies suddenly and the parents ask why. A young husband is killed by a drunk driver, and his wife and small children ask why. No words can answer that anguishing question.

Where is God when it hurts? Sometimes it seems He is silent just when we need Him most. Why do suffering and pain afflict good people? In my opinion, there are three basic reasons.

Reality Therapy

• Because of poor choices. A young man came to my office for counseling. His left arm had been cut off just above the elbow in an auto accident. During our session he began to vent his anger toward God because he was not a whole man. He had lost his job and his appearance was marred because, he believed, he was a cripple.

When I pressed for details, I learned he was the driver in a single-car accident. He was drunk, driving like a wild man, and plowed into a massive oak tree. I decided to administer a stiff dose of reality therapy.

"Your arm was cut off because you chose to drive while drunk," I said. "God didn't pour the whiskey down your throat. He didn't force you into the driver's seat and out onto the highway. *You chose* to do those things. You made a series of poor choices, and the consequences are yours to bear." Then I went on to share with him how God could help him deal redemptively with those consequences.

Taking Responsibility

People who are suffering are seldom willing to acknowledge their responsibility in the matter. I have begged young women in my church not to marry the young men they were seeing until their professions of faith manifested some fruit. Ignoring God's clear warning not to be unequally yoked with unbelievers, they prance up the aisle smiling. Months or years later they're in the courtroom crying. Their suffering isn't God's fault. It's the product of poor choice.

I have implored businessmen not to join in contracts with questionable unbelievers. But in mad pursuit of the chance of a lifetime, they plunge into a financial abyss that destroys their credit, their good name, the future of their children and sometimes even their health. I have heard them ask, "Why is God letting this happen to me?" The answer is, It isn't God who's making this happen. It's the consequence of your poor choices.

The Light of Knowledge

• Because of ignorance. Knowledge is power. In July 1881, President James A. Garfield was shot by an assassin. He died two months later—because his doctors couldn't agree on the location of the bullet in his body (they had no X-ray in those days). Garfield's personal physician, Dr. Bliss, was certain the bullet was in one area. A specialist, Dr. Weiss, insisted it was in another.

The two doctors argued back and forth. The result? No operation, and the president died. When the autopsy later showed that Dr. Weiss had been correct, a Washington newspaper quipped, "Ignorance Is Bliss."

It makes a cute saying. But it's utterly false. What we don't know can hurt us and bring us pain and suffering. Knowledge is a God-given light that can steer us away from the deep ditches of disaster.

God's Sovereignty

• Because of the sovereign, long-range purposes of God. There are times when things happen over which we have no control and about which we can have no knowledge. We pound on heaven's gates, asking, Why is this happening? And in response we hear only the deafening sound of eternal silence.

When Joseph's brothers sold him into slavery in Egypt, it seemed the darkest day of his life. One moment he was the favorite son of his father, Jacob. The next moment he was bouncing along on the back of a mangy camel en route to a nightmare in Egypt. He couldn't possibly have understood at that moment the long-range purposes of God in his life, or comprehended how the hand of God was directing every agonizing step.

Steel in the Soul

But the fiery trial of tragedy forged steel in Joseph's soul. The pain of rejection and loneliness forged the golden chain that Pharaoh placed around his neck, making him "prime minister" of Egypt.

Seventeen years later, when starvation drove his brothers into Egypt in search of food, Joseph began to see what God had in mind the day He allowed Joseph's brothers to sell him into slavery. Only when Joseph saw his aged father and all his kin settled in the rich lands of Goshen did he fully grasp what God had been up to since day one.

From Sorrow to Singing

When our hearts are breaking and our eyes are blinded with tears, it's hard to see the sovereign hand of God guiding our every step. We suffer until the purposes of God become apparent to us, which may not happen for many years and may not be at all in this life.

But if we endure to the end and run the race that is set before us with patience, our tears will turn to joy and our sorrow into singing. We who mourn will be comforted. God guarantees it.

6

Happiness Comes
Through Meekness

Happy are the meek,
for they shall inherit the earth.

Jesus, the master architect of the soul, establishes in detail the steps we must take to be happy in an unhappy world. He reveals the blueprint of happiness for all men and women to follow for all time.

First, as we've seen, there must be brokenness before God. Second, there must be mourning for wrongdoing. And third, there must be meekness.

A Hardball Society

Happy are the meek. Does that sound absurd? In our hardball society, meekness is considered a liability, not an asset.

We've all heard the gospel according to Leo Durocher: Nice guys finish last.

Our society believes the way to inherit is to be mean as a junkyard dog. We've all seen those little plaques that say, "If you love something, let it go; if it does not return to you, hunt it down and kill it," and "If you don't like the way I drive, stay off the sidewalk." But when did you last see a plaque that said, "Happy are the meek"?

The Meek Messiah

Remember to whom Jesus is speaking. At this point, the Jews are living under severe political oppression. Since 63 B.C. they have lived under a series of brutal rulers appointed by Rome. One of them, Herod the Great, executed nine of his ten wives merely on the suspicion of infidelity. He issued standing orders that his son was to be executed the day he died—so that at least someone would mourn his passing. The Jews had a saying: better to be Herod's swine than his son.

Jesus' listeners are looking desperately for a messiah who will crush Roman imperialism. The legalistic Pharisees want a messiah of miracles. The liberal Sadducees want a materialistic messiah. The Essenes are looking for a monastic messiah. The political-activist Zealots, who want to send their tormentors back to Rome in body bags, want a military messiah.

Meekness or Weakness?

So what happens? Along comes Jesus of Nazareth, whose teachings and miracles have aroused the entire nation. Anticipation builds among the people. Could this be the promised messiah? They hang on His every word. He continues the Magna Carta of Happiness by saying, "Happy are the meek...."

A man in the crowd throws up his hands and says to his

friends, "Can you believe this guy? Get serious! You don't conquer Romans with meekness. You don't come to a cold-blooded killer like Herod with hat in hand. Happy are the meek? Nonsense! Might makes right! Meekness is weakness!"

God's Gentlemen

But meekness is *not* weakness. In his commentary on the book of Matthew (Revell), Matthew Henry said, "The meek are those who quietly submit themselves before God, to His Word, to His rod, who follow His directions and comply with His designs and are gentle toward men."

The meek are God's gentlemen. They are not intimidated by loud-mouthed mental midgets. They are cool and calm in adversity. They have warm hearts, not hot heads.

Our culture has rejected meekness as a principle of happiness. This rejection of meekness creates a vacuum filled with barbaric behavior. We don't want to hear about meekness. Give us Rambo!

We don't want to hear the voice of the Holy Spirit whisper, "The fruit of the Spirit is love, joy, peace, long-suffering, gentleness, goodness, faith, meekness and temperance" (Gal. 5:22-23, KJV). We have rejected meekness as a path to happiness.

What then? Does being meek mean we allow the aggressive to run over us? Does it mean we stand silent, head bowed, while being verbally abused? No. Meekness speaks the truth in love. It stands its ground calmly and resolutely. We can stand against injustice with anointed fury and still be meek.

Moses: Champion of Meekness

Consider Moses, the Old Testament's champion of meekness. The Bible says, "Now Moses was a very humble man,

more humble than anyone else on the face of the earth"
(Num. 12:3).

He was meek. But was he weak? See him slay the Egyp-
tian who is beating his Hebrew brother unjustly. See him
flee to the desert and amass a fortune over forty years. See
him face mighty Pharaoh and demand, "Let my people go!"
See him lead a horde of escaped slaves across a desert
wasteland for forty years, to a land flowing with milk and
honey.

When God becomes angry with Israel—so much so that
He is ready to slay them to the last man—see Moses stand
in intercession and say, "If you kill them, Lord, kill me too!"
God changes His mind because of Moses. That's meekness.
But it's anything but weakness.

Paul: Model of Meekness

Or consider the apostle Paul as a model of meekness. Paul
wrote:

• "I therefore, the prisoner of the Lord, beseech you that
ye walk worthy of the vocation wherewith ye are called, with
all lowliness and meekness, with longsuffering, forbearing
one another in love" (Eph. 4:1-2, KJV).

• "To speak evil of no man, to be no brawlers, but gentle, showing all meekness unto all men" (Titus 3:2, KJV).

• "Put on therefore, as the elect of God, holy and beloved,
bowels of mercies, kindness, humbleness of mind, meekness,
longsuffering" (Col. 3:12, KJV).

Paul instructed Timothy to pursue meekness (1 Tim. 6:11).
Timothy was to *pursue* meekness. He was not to rest until
he had enriched his character with this priceless virtue.

Paul was meek. But was he weak? When on the isle of
Malta, he shook a deadly viper from his wrist as men gasped
in wonder. When dragged into court, he glared at his persecutors and said, "God will strike you, you whitewashed

wall!'' (Acts 23:3). When, in jail, the jailers discovered he was a Roman citizen and tried to release him secretly, Paul said, ''Oh, no, you don't! You put me in here publicly and you're going to let me out publicly. Go get the mayor, the city council and Ted Koppel. *Then* let me out!'' He was meek. But he was anything but weak.

Jesus: Meek But Not Weak

Or consider Christ Jesus our Lord, who said, ''Learn of me; for I am meek and lowly in heart'' (Matt. 11:29, KJV).

See the Son of God as He invades the temple with a whip of cords, His eyes blazing with righteous indignation, crying, ''It is written,...'My house will be called a house of prayer,' but you are making it a 'den of robbers' '' (Matt. 21:13).

Hear Him rebuke the Pharisees: ''You snakes! You brood of vipers! How will you escape being condemned to hell?'' (Matt. 23:33).

Watch as Roman guards slap His face and mock Him, saying, ''Hail, king of the Jews!'' (Matt. 27:29). He does not revile them in return, but bears insult with dignity.

Listen to the cat-o'-nine-tails slash through the air, ripping His back to shreds. Look to Calvary, where He willingly lets His hands and feet be nailed to the cursed cross.

See Him now, seated at the right hand of God the Father, the ultimate position of power in all the cosmos. When He returns to the earth, He will rule the nations with a rod of iron. He is meek. But He is anything but weak.

Mastery of Self

Meekness is mastery of self. The Bible says, ''Better a patient man than a warrior, a man who controls his temper than one who takes a city'' (Prov. 16:32).

A college president made this statement to a class of

graduating seniors: "It gets easier and easier for man to control his universe, and harder and harder for him to control himself."

Can you control yourself? A woman once said to me, "Pastor, sometimes I lose my temper. But it's no big deal. It's over in three minutes."

I said, "So is a tornado! But it takes days to bury the dead, weeks to assess the damage and years to recover the loss. Do your family a favor and learn to control yourself!"

Meekness in Marriage

Wife, are you meek toward your husband? Or do you pride yourself on your ability to manipulate him? Your husband is the God-ordained leader of your house. If you cut him to shreds, your marriage will be destroyed and your children will rise up and curse you. I know he may not be the most dynamic man in the world. But he's the one you chose, the one to whom you pledged your love and loyalty.

Husband, are you meek toward your wife? The Bible doesn't say, "Husband, change your wife." It says, "Husband, love your wife and honor her as the weaker vessel." Marriage will not work without meekness from both parties. It began when Adam took a nap and woke up married. God didn't take a bone from Adam's head, that the woman might rule over him, nor did He take a bone from his foot, that he might tread on her. God took a bone from Adam's side so that the love of his life could walk next to him as an equal partner.

Meekness in the Family and the Church

Parents, are you meek toward your children? The Bible says, "Fathers, do not exasperate your children" (Eph. 6:4). Do you make unreasonable demands of your children? Do you try to relive your life through them? Are your expectations of them within bounds?

Are you meek toward your brothers and sisters in Christ? Or are you incessantly critical of others? Do you know that Satan criticizes the saints of God before His throne day and night? The Bible calls him "the accuser of our brothers" (Rev. 12:10). When you criticize another member of the body of Christ, you are doing the work of Satan himself. Ask God to crucify your critical spirit and give you a spirit of meekness and quietness.

A missionary in Africa once came upon some boys playing a game of marbles—using real diamonds. He couldn't believe his eyes. There in the dust lay a fortune—priceless possessions considered to be of no value whatever. So it is with us and the priceless treasure of meekness. God says, "It's a pearl of great price." The world says, "Who needs it?"

The Alternative to Meekness

Meekness enables us to be led by the Spirit of God. James tells of the alternative when he writes of the necessity of putting bits in the mouths of horses to force them to obey us (see James 3:3).

I own a farm on which I once kept a semi-broken quarter-horse named Bucky. I didn't ride Bucky often, and when I did there was ongoing conflict as to who was really in charge.

One fine spring day I saddled Bucky for one of our infrequent jaunts around the farm. As soon as my backside touched the saddle, I had the violent sensation of being launched from Cape Canaveral—minus countdown and rocket!

I hit the ground like a sack of salt. I could almost see that horse laugh at me. I gave Bucky a good cuff behind the ears and delivered part one of my three-part series on submission to authority.

The Spanish Bit

An experienced cowboy who witnessed the scene told me, "Preacher, you've got the wrong kind of bit in that horse's mouth. You need a Spanish bit."

"What good will that do?" I asked, rubbing my sore hind quarters.

"If he doesn't obey right away when you tug on the reins, it will cut his mouth to the quick. It's a bit harsh, but it won't do any lasting damage. And he'll learn to obey right quick."

Needless to say, I wasted little time getting one of those marvelous Spanish bits for my stubborn horse. It worked like a charm. Bucky instantly obeyed my every command.

As I dismounted I could almost hear the Lord say, "Many of My children are so stubborn they force Me to put bits into their mouths that cut them to the quick. If they would just be meek and let Me guide them by the voice of My Spirit, how happy they would be!" But so often we refuse meekness, demand our own way and forfeit the happiness God has in mind for us.

The Meek Shall Inherit the Earth

When Jesus said this, He was quoting King David: "The meek will inherit the land and enjoy great peace" (Ps. 37:11). The violent try to take the earth by force. But "the earth is the Lord's, and everything in it" (Ps. 24:1). As owner, He can will it to whomever He pleases. And He has already made out the title deed to planet Earth to the meek.

There are two meanings to this. The first is a natural meaning. Jesus is talking to Jews living under Roman occupation. He is saying, "You will inherit the land of Israel as promised to Abraham." God's covenant with Abraham was an unconditional and everlasting covenant, established solely on the faithfulness of God.

Sand and Stars

Abraham is identified in Scripture as "the father of all who believe" (Rom. 4:11). Scripture describes his descendants as the "sand on the seashore" and as the "stars in the sky" (see Gen. 22:17). The sand represents Israel and the stars represent the church.

Stars are first mentioned in the very first chapter of Genesis, where they are described as having three functions. They give light, they rule the night and they divide light from darkness. So it is with the church. The church gives light: "You are the light of the world," Jesus said (Matt. 5:14). The church rules: We are given dominion over all things in the name of Jesus. And the church is the dividing element between light and darkness: We are either for Christ or against Him, either saved or lost.

Sand is earthly; stars are heavenly. There is an earthly Jerusalem, ruled by the Jewish people, and a New Jerusalem in the heavens, ruled by the church. Both have their place and function, and neither replaces the other in the economy of God.

So in one sense Jesus was looking through the telescope of prophecy, telling His audience, "The day is coming when I will restore the land of Israel to the Jewish people."

Jesus' Return

But there is also a spiritual meaning of "they shall inherit the earth." For Jesus Christ is coming to earth again. He will literally rule this earth for a thousand years. When He returns, the meek will inherit the earth.

The first time He came, He was a babe in Bethlehem's manger. The next time He comes, He will be King of kings and Lord of lords.

The first time He came, He rode into Jerusalem on the

foal of an ass. The next time He comes, He will split the heavens riding a white horse, as a mighty conqueror.

The first time He came, He was dragged before Pilate. The next time He comes, Pilate will bow down before Him and confess that He is Lord.

The first time He came, He was crucified on the cross. The next time He comes, He will sit on the throne of His father David and rule the earth with a rod of iron.

Only the meek can inherit the earth. Happiness comes when meekness is accepted as the third principle of being happy in an unhappy world. Our society has planted the seeds of violence and has reaped the whirlwind. It's time to plant seeds of meekness and reap a harvest of happiness!

7

Happiness Comes Through Hunger and Thirst

Happy are those who hunger and thirst after righteousness,
for they shall be filled.

Jesus' Magna Carta of Happiness dramatically demonstrates that happiness is inward. It's living life "from the inside out." Happiness begins by allowing the architect of the ages to place our life on His potter's wheel to mold and make us according to His design.

In the beginning, the hand of God scooped up a handful of clay, molded it, breathed life into it, and man became a living soul. Today, when we come to Him battered, blemished and broken, He places our clay frame upon His wheel, breaks us, remakes us and releases us as a vessel of perfection, beauty and honor. The next time you look in the mirror, tell yourself confidently, "God doesn't manufacture junk, and He doesn't sponsor flops. I'm an original expression of God's creative genius."

We've already seen that happiness requires that we be broken in spirit, which leads to mourning for wrongdoing and then to the quality of meekness. Now we are ready for the final inward condition for happiness: what Jesus calls hunger and thirst for righteousness.

Right Living

In the sixteenth century, when the majestic King James version of the Bible was being put together, righteousness meant "rightwise," or "as it ought to be." We can think of it simply as "right living."

Righteousness is right living according to God's standard of holiness. "Be holy," says the Lord, "because I am holy" (1 Pet. 1:16). Our standards of right living are not to be chosen by the herd instinct of our humanistic society. Humanism has defied man and demoted God to a cosmic bellhop responding to our patronizing tips. Humanistic society states, "I am the captain of my soul and the master of my fate." But God has published His standard of righteousness in the Word of God, the Bible.

God's Standards

The United States government has a National Bureau of Standards in Washington, D.C. It sets the standards for weights and measures all over the country. It guarantees that a pound of bologna weighs sixteen ounces whether you order it in Texas or Florida. Distance, time and public opinion do not affect the National Bureau of Standards.

The Bible is the ultimate standard of righteousness for all people all over the world. What is sin in Texas is sin in Florida, in Europe, in Africa, in Asia and everywhere else

Distance, time and public opinion do not affect God's standard of righteousness. "In the gospel," writes Paul, "a righteousness from God is revealed" (Rom. 1:17).

The Garments of Righteousness

What attitude should the church take toward a sin-saturated world that protests against God's standard of righteousness as being "out of step with the times"? Shall we lower the standard of righteousness so that immoral and godless rogues can sit with comfort in the house of God?

The truth is, it's not in our power to lower the standard of righteousness. God has forever established that standard on earth through the life of Jesus Christ. Those who profess to lower the standard to appease complacent congregations are hirelings, not shepherds. They are preaching a false gospel.

Righteousness is not living "just a cut above" the pagan next door. It's right living according to the Word of God. The garments of righteousness never go out of style. God never alters the robe of righteousness to fit the man. Rather He alters the man to fit the robe. God doesn't have "different strokes for different folks." Time, distance or changes in public attitudes do not alter God's standard of righteousness one iota.

"Restrained Righteousness"

The Japanese have a saying that a snake lies straight as long as it's kept inside a bamboo stick. When released, it starts wiggling and acting "snaky" again.

Many people have what I call restrained righteousness. As long as they are forced by external restraints to be as they ought to be, they appear to be righteous. But when the exterior restraints are removed, their genuine character is revealed. They start acting snaky.

• Physical force is an obvious form of external restraint. When I was a child, my conduct was kept "as it ought to be" by my father's leather strap. It didn't make me hunger and thirst after righteousness, but it sure made me desire not to get caught. When I was away from the house, I started acting snaky again.

• Legalism is an external restraint. Legalism is a man-made religious system structured around rules and regulations and enforced by peer pressure. But following man-made rules and regulations doesn't constitute the righteousness of God. "All our righteous acts are like filthy rags," writes Isaiah (64:6).

Saintly or Snaky?

• There is the restraint of associations. When we are hemmed in by a close circle of friends who live righteously, we can hardly do anything but go along with their behavior. We're like barrel staves held in place by hoops of steel. But what are we like when we leave town for two weeks and go to a place where no one knows us? Do we then start acting snaky?

• There is the restraint of tasks. I have known people to function in the church because they had a titled position. When they leave the position, they collapse like a house of cards. They quit the church and start acting snaky.

The true test of our righteousness comes when the restraints are lifted. Do we act saintly or snaky? Catalog your own actions and activities. Would you like them to be published in your hometown newspaper? What does that tell you about how much you really hunger and thirst after righteousness?

Desperate Longing

The Greek verbs used by Jesus in this fourth principle of happiness are very powerful. We are to *peinao* and *dipsao* after righteousness. *Peinao* means to suffer deep hunger. *Dipsao* means to be consumed with thirst. The point? Only when we are consumed with desperate longing for righteousness will we be happy!

A young man asked his pastor how to be happy. The pastor said, "Come with me. I'll show you how to find happiness." They walked to the river, where the young man assumed he would probably get baptized.

When they were chest-deep in the river, the pastor suddenly grabbed the young man's head and forced it under the water. The young man thrashed about violently, convinced he was going to drown. At last he managed to get his head above water and gasp for air.

The pastor looked him in the eye and said, "Young man, when you hunger and thirst after righteousness as desperately as you craved air just now—*then* happiness will be yours."

Signs of Life

It is a biological fact that every living thing hungers and thirsts.

I have five healthy children who are the joy of my life. When I brought them home from the hospital, they came through the door hungry and thirsty. Any of them would—and at one time or another all of them did—wake me up without hesitation at all hours of the night to demand food. They didn't care that I'd just gone to bed after an emergency pastoral call. They didn't care that they'd single-handedly destroyed my sleep five nights in a row. They just knew they were hungry and they wanted food *now*.

To tell you the truth, those midnight cries were music to

my ears. It meant the kids were healthy and growing. I knew as I stumbled down the dark hallway with another bottle that those cries were evidence of vibrant life.

Only the dead and the dying are without appetite. They want no food. They crave no water. When we feel bad and go to the doctor, the first question he asks us is, "How's your appetite?" Loss of appetite is nature's way of telling us we're sick.

Jesus was asking His audience by the Sea of Galilee—and our hedonistic generation as well—"How's your appetite for right living?"

We Are What We Eat

Do you know the expression "You are what you eat"? I don't know if it's true in the physical realm, but it's certainly true in the spiritual realm. If we eat the wrong spiritual foods, we're not going to feel well or be happy. If we take in negative, hateful and loveless thoughts, we're guaranteed to be miserable. If we watch television and take in several savage murders salted with hatred, revenge and rebellion, and peppered with greed and lust, we're surely not going to feel too happy.

Then when we go to church on Sunday morning, we turn up our noses. The hymns don't appeal to us. When we hear the pure Word of God, we're not interested. It's milk for newborn Christians and meat for mature saints, but we push it away.

Why? Simple! We can't eat slop all week and feel like a saint on Sunday morning. It's impossible. God's standard of righteousness won't permit it.

Heaven or Hell on Earth?

I read of a man who went to a professional football game

one Sunday afternoon. To his dismay, he found himself on the bus sitting between two men who were on their way home from church. They were talking about how God answers prayer and discussing the joy and happiness of knowing Christ and enjoying His presence in their homes and marriages.

When the man got off at the stadium, he told his friends, "I got stuck on the bus between two guys talking about God answering prayer and going to heaven and all that stuff. I was sure in one hell of a fix!"

There you have it! What was heaven for two saints was hell on earth for him. He had no appetite for it. He was spiritually sick.

When we lack appetite for spiritual things, which is the basis of happiness, it's not because we're too sophisticated or too intellectual to accept God's standard of righteousness. It's because we're too spiritually anemic to know we're dying.

Righteousness Exalts a Nation

America hungers and thirsts for everything but righteousness. We hunger for drink, drugs, sex and material things. Greed is the spirit of the age. We want more, more, more.

Our youth are turning to Satanism and witchcraft. Abortion clinics have become our scientific Auschwitz. Medical experts predict that twenty million of us will be dying from AIDS by the year 2000. Economists write about the collapse of capitalism that could result from the loss of an entire generation that has been killed by abortion or by AIDS.

How has all this befallen us? It is the direct result of our appetite. It's time to hunger and thirst after righteousness. It's time to heed the Word of God:

> If my people, who are called by my name,
> will humble themselves and pray and seek my
> face and turn from their wicked ways, then

will I hear from heaven and will forgive their
sin and will heal their land (2 Chron. 7:14).

Righteousness exalts a nation, but sin is
a disgrace to any people (Prov. 14:34).

Righteous Responsibility

The secret of happiness lies not in doing what we want
to do but in doing what we ought to do. Happiness never
comes to the person who dodges responsibility. Franklin D.
Roosevelt once said, "Happiness is the joy of achievement
and the thrill of creative effort." There is nothing in the world
that helps a man overcome his difficulties, survive his
disasters, and stay healthy and happy like the joy of a life's
task worthy of his full dedication.

Righteous responsibility is a mark of spiritual maturity.
We don't serve the Lord by feeling or emotion, but by duty
and devotion. There is no happiness without righteous responsibility.

Producing or Consuming?

Responsibility comes by degrees with advancing maturity. In the natural realm, maturity can be measured by whether
we are producing more than we consume. When children
are small, all they know how to do is consume. As they
mature they begin to become responsible and productive
through simple tasks like carrying out the trash and clean-
ing up their rooms.

Then comes the day when you say something radical like,
"It's time for you to get a job!" They look at you, pained
and puzzled, and say something profound like, "Me? Go
to work? Get serious!"

After they recover from the shock, they get a job that covers
some of their consumption. Eventually they will be able to

pay their own way. And by the grace of God, someday they'll be able to support not only themselves but also a wife and children.

Spiritual Maturity

Spiritual maturity works much the same way. We must grow to a point where we produce more than we consume. The church is flooded with spiritually immature creatures who come to church, take in the delicious Word of God, absorb the beautiful music, enjoy the delightful fellowship—and then go swiftly out the door to do absolutely nothing. They don't witness to the lost. They don't pray. They don't give. They could sing in the choir, but they won't. They could serve, but they won't.

When we're in this condition, we don't rise to our righteous responsibility. The time has come, after years of consuming, to start being productive for the kingdom. It's time to put our hands to the plow, to become fruitful servants in the Lord's vineyard. Life is God's gift to us. What we do with it is our gift to Him. What are we doing with our lives? Are we growing toward maturity by being productive? Or are we stalled in a consumer mode?

A Road to Nowhere

Novelist George Moore tells of Irish peasants during the Depression put to work by the government building roads. For a time they work hard, singing under the hot sun, happy to be employed again.

But little by little they realize the road they are building leads nowhere. They have been put to work merely to give the government a rationale for feeding them. They grow listless. Their singing stops.

"The roads to nowhere are difficult to make," writes Moore.

"For a man to work well and sing, there must be an end in view."

What about you? Are you on a road to nowhere? Have you consumed the good things of God without giving your time and talent in return?

Can't or Won't

Is your hunger for the things of God conditional? Do you say, I want to live a righteous life and know real happiness, but—

I can't forgive my husband.

I can't forgive my wife.

I can't stop lying and cheating.

I can't give up my mistress.

I can't give up my greed and materialism.

Wrong! You *can* do all of the above. You just won't! If you want to be happy, stop saying, "I can't," and start saying, "I will."

"They Shall Be Filled"

"Filled" is a fantastic word. It means "absolutely satisfied." Overflowing with God's good, old-fashioned, heart-warming happiness. David wrote, "He satisfies the thirsty and fills the hungry with good things" (Ps. 107:9).

A twelve-year-old girl from the slums of Chicago was rushed to the hospital, diagnosed as having double pneumonia. Hospital administrators put her story together and discovered she was scrubbing floors twelve hours a day to support her mother and her four brothers and sisters. In the bitter cold of winter she had developed pneumonia and was terribly underweight from malnutrition.

One day a nurse brought her a glass of milk. The girl looked up and asked, "How much can I have?"

"What do you mean, honey?" asked the nurse.

"The milk. How much can I have?"

"Why, all of it, of course," replied the nurse. "Why do you ask?"

"Because at my house we draw a line on the glass. You can only drink to the line, and then you have to pass the glass to someone else."

"Your Soul Will Delight"

The Bible says, "Come, all you who are thirsty, come to the waters; and you who have no money, come, buy and eat! Come, buy wine and milk without money and without cost. Why spend money on what is not bread, and your labor on what does not satisfy? Listen, listen to me, and eat what is good, and your soul will delight in the richest of fare" (Is. 55:1-2). God doesn't draw a line on the glass.

Are you looking for real happiness? When you hunger and thirst after righteousness as desperately as a drowning man craves air, you'll find it. It's not just feeling; it's living faith. It's not sensation; it's salvation. It's not religion; it's righteousness through responsibility. Happy are those who hunger and thirst after righteousness, for they shall be filled.

8

Happiness Comes Through Mercy

Happy are the merciful,
for they shall obtain mercy.

The principles in Jesus' Magna Carta of Happiness are radical. They seem utterly unworkable. We don't readily grasp the connection between mourning, meekness and mercy. How can that combination possibly bring anyone happiness?

The first four principles deal with the inner man. First we are broken in spirit. Then we mourn over the sinful conduct of our life. Then we embrace meekness. All this produces a deep hunger and thirst for righteousness.

The first outward demonstration of what has been happening inwardly comes in the form of mercy. Mercy is the first external evidence the world can observe to verify that God is at work on the inside.

A Merciful Church

If Satan can remove mercy from the conduct of Christians, the church will die. If we become so busy with buildings, budgets and baptisms that we lose compassion for the suffering stream of humanity that flows through our doors, we may as well close our doors.

If there is no mercy in the house of God, then the glory of the Lord is departed. There is no peace, no joy, no love. Without mercy the church is a tree with no fruit. It's a well without water. It's a cloud without rain. Without mercy, the church becomes nothing more than a religious country club. The building should be burned to the ground before the congregation gets sued for false advertising!

The Greek word for merciful is *eleemon*, which means "to be beneficial." It's God's will that every church be beneficial to those who walk through its doors. Those attending should go home in a better condition than the one in which they came, from having been in the presence of God's mercy.

The church is a healing force in a hurting world. It's a hospital for the battered and broken. It's a fortress of faith in a world of doubt and skepticism. It's a house of comfort where hope is reborn. It's a place of worship where God is revered, where His Word is proclaimed and where His Son, Jesus, is Lord.

Mercy Is Appealing

Of all the principles of happiness that Jesus proclaims, this one is the most appealing, the most important and the most difficult.

It's appealing because we all crave mercy. This is especially true, for instance, when we're clocked by radar doing fifty miles per hour in a thirty-five-mile-per-hour zone. Before we have the window rolled all the way down we're pleading for mercy. "Officer, something must be terribly wrong with my speedometer," we say, "because this is the second one of these I've gotten today."

"Here's the third," replies the officer in a monotone. "One more of these and you'll be riding a bicycle."

Mercy is very appealing. And the more we recognize how desperately we need it, the more appealing it is.

Mercy Is Important

It's important because it's *prima facie* evidence that we are becoming like God the Father. We are never more like God than when we are showing mercy.

> Can a mother forget the baby at her breast and have no compassion on the child she has borne? Though she may forget, I will not forget you! (Is. 49:15).

Mothers in Africa throw their newborn babies to the crocodiles. Mothers in India watch their babies starve in the shadow of a fat cow considered too sacred to eat. Mothers in America abort their babies to appease the god of self. But our heavenly Father is full of mercy toward us:

> It is of the Lord's *mercies* that we are not consumed, because his compassions fail not. They are new every morning; great is thy faithfulness (Lam. 3:22-23, KJV, italics added).

> Surely goodness and *mercy* shall follow me all the days of my life: and I will dwell in the house of the Lord for ever (Ps. 23:6, KJV, italics added).

> The Lord is full of compassion and *mercy* (James 5:11, italics added).

Meeting a Need

Last Christmas, a gracious lady at Cornerstone Church approached my wife, Diana, and told her she had a new ten-speed bicycle she wasn't using and she wanted to give it to someone who needed it. Diana thanked her, shook her hand and started to walk away. She hadn't taken three steps when she was stopped by a physician who had brought a twelve-year-old boy to church for the very first time.

Diana didn't know that the boy was the sole support of his mother and sisters. He had come to church that day to ask God to help him better provide for them. Specifically, he needed—you guessed it—a bicycle so he could get a paper route to help feed his family.

On Christmas Eve, our church's custom is to take baskets filled with fruit, vegetables, turkeys and candies to families that otherwise wouldn't have them. That very day the little boy's mother had been going from place to place looking for food to feed her children for Christmas. When the baskets from the church arrived, she burst into tears.

Dancing for Joy

While the family danced for joy in the middle of the room, our church representative said, "We have something else for you, too." They all ran outside to see the new ten-speed bicycle tied to the roof of the car. That little boy threw his arms around his mother, crying, "See, Mama? I told you Jesus would answer my prayers! And He did!"

Do you know what happiness is? It's watching a family dance for joy at having food to eat on Christmas Day. It's watching a twelve-year-old boy hug a bicycle with tears of thankfulness in his eyes.

Happy are the merciful. Happy are those who dare to show kindness in a cold, jaded world. Happy are those moved by compassion to action. These are the people who shall obtain mercy from the God of all mercy.

Mercy Is Difficult

It's difficult for us to show mercy because we are inherently lovers of self. Selfishness short-circuits prayer and tarnishes everything it touches. A man wrapped in himself makes a mighty small package. A man who is self-centered is off-centered.

Mercy requires that we learn to love others, to value their welfare more than our own.

Mercy Always Manifests Itself

A man can have money in his pocket and not show it. He can have the musical skill of Beethoven and not reveal it. He can have the knowledge of Einstein and not expose it. But if a man has the loving mercy of the living God in his soul, he can't help but manifest it.

He can't hide it. When he sees a brother in distress, he can no more turn his head and walk away than the sun can refuse to shine at noonday. It's impossible.

Giving to the Poor

The Bible says, "Defend the cause of the weak and fatherless; maintain the rights of the poor and oppressed" (Ps. 82:3). Why? "If a man shuts his ears to the cry of the poor, he too will cry out and not be answered" (Prov. 21:13).

Jesus said, "Give to the one who asks you, and do not turn away from the one who wants to borrow from you" (Matt. 5:42). And later He said, "Give, and it will be given to you. A good measure, pressed down, shaken together and running over, will be poured into your lap" (Luke 6:38).

George Mueller was walking past an orphanage in London

when he saw, sticking through a picket fence, the dirty hand of a ragged little girl. At that time orphans, lunatics and criminals were all thrown into one massive compound of human suffering.

That dirty little hand, pleading wordlessly through the fence, would not leave Mueller's mind. His heart was stirred to action as the Holy Spirit directed him to do all he could to show mercy toward the pitiful orphans of England.

A Divine Assignment

He discussed the matter with his wife, and they decided to open the doors of their home in a living demonstration of mercy. Their faith pledge to each other was "the day the Lord stops providing the food and finances for these children, we stop."

They promptly filled their home with orphans. Without support from a single local church or government agency, they determined to give their all in this divine assignment. They sold the beautiful silver service and heirloom china they had received as wedding gifts. They stripped themselves of their wealth in absolute determination to provide for these unwanted and unloved children.

Daily Miracles

God supernaturally supplied the needs of the Muellers on a day-to-day basis with miracle after miracle. When there was no food, Mueller would have the children fold their hands and give thanks for food that wasn't there. Before the prayer was ended, food would arrive from a merchant or business-man whom God had moved to provide for the children.

George Mueller filled his own house with orphans, then the house next door, and the next house, and the next, until the neighbors protested that the children were taking over the neighborhood. Mueller asked God for an answer. The next day he saw a beautiful piece of property. "The orphanage will be built there," he said. He was told the property belonged to the government and was absolutely unavailable. Six weeks later George Mueller owned the property and began building the most spectacular orphanage England had ever seen.

At age seventy-three, when most men are concerned with personal comfort and retirement, George Mueller was still housing, feeding, clothing and educating 2,500 orphans without one dime of support from church or state.

Mercy Is Manifested in Serving

The measure of a man's greatness is not the number of servants he has, but the number of people he serves. History proves that the only great men among us are those who serve.

The apostle Paul was a servant to God and man. Nero was a rich, powerful, self-centered monarch who ruled Rome. We name our sons Paul. We name our dogs Nero!

Mercy Is Manifested in Forgiveness

Peer Holm was a world-famous engineer. He built bridges, railroads and tunnels in many parts of the world and gained wealth and fame, but later came to failure, poverty and sickness. He returned to the little village where he was born and, together with his wife and little daughter, eked out a meager living.

Peer Holm had a neighbor who owned a fierce dog. Peer warned him that the dog was dangerous, but the old man contemptuously replied, "Hold your tongue, you cursed pauper."

One day Holm found the dog at the throat of his little girl. He did all he could to tear the dog away, but it was too late. The dog's teeth had sunk too deeply. The little girl died.

Mercy Triumphs Over Bitterness

The sheriff shot the dog, and the neighbors were bitter against the owner. When sowing time came, they refused to sell him grain. His fields were plowed but bare. He couldn't beg, borrow or buy seed. Whenever he walked down the road, the people of the village sneered at him.

But not Peer Holm. He could not sleep at night for worrying about his neighbor. Early one morning he rose, went to his shed and took out his last half-bushel of barley. He climbed the fence and sowed his neighbor's field.

The fields themselves told the story. When the seeds sprouted, it was clear what Peer Holm had done, because a part of his field remained bare while his neighbor's field was green. His act of forgiveness manifested mercy in a dramatic way.

Restoring Fallen Brothers

Paul writes, "Brothers, if someone is caught in a sin, you who are spiritual should restore him gently" (Gal. 6:1).

Mercy searches for a way to restore a fallen friend. The calloused heart will sneer, He got what he deserved! The heart that has been crushed on the potter's wheel asks, What can I do to help? One hug can make the difference between a heart that breaks and a heart that heals.

When Paul first wrote to the believers at Corinth, he rebuked them for sexual misconduct, mismanagement of church funds and getting drunk at communion. You don't need a seminary degree to know those are some pretty serious sins.

But in his second letter, Paul writes, "I have great confidence in you" (2 Cor. 7:4). Think of it! Paul puts his fatherly arms around those champion sinners, with an encouraging word for their reformation and restoration.

Mercy Is Greater Than Sympathy

Sympathy is an emotion. It's often accompanied by tears. There are those who weep so easily their tears are meaningless. It's all right to weep, of course, but genuine mercy requires a willingness to act.

Jesus wept. But He did far more. He acted. He went to the cross and died to save those for whom He wept.

If your brother has genuine need of twenty dollars, and you have forty dollars in your pocket, don't just "pray about it"—give him twenty bucks. If you see a sister whose dress is threadbare, don't just utter a sympathetic comment in her direction—give her one of your dresses.

Mercy Is Greater Than Prejudice

Prejudice means "prejudging," or making an evaluation of others before we know all the facts. Prejudice is a mark of mental, moral and spiritual weakness. The prejudiced person believes there are two sides to every question: his side and the wrong side. Prejudice is a form of robbery: It robs the victim of a fair trial in the court of reason. Prejudice is murder: It kills the opportunity for advancement for those who are its prey.

The church is riddled with prejudice. That sounds harsh, but it's true. Racial prejudice is still alive and well in many places. Religious prejudice abounds. Many people are far more proud of their religion than they are of Jesus. There is economic prejudice. But let me tell you, ma'am, that when you kneel to pray in your satin designer dress, the housemaid who kneels beside you is also the beloved daughter of the Lord. And you, sir, when you fold your diamond-studded fingers to pray, the man beside you whose hands are covered with calluses is also a son of God.

Mercy and Might

Jesus was mighty. He was merciful. Mercy drove Him from the balconies of a perfect heaven to a sin-saturated earth. It was tender pity for humanity in its sin, its misery, its darkness and its hopelessness that moved His heart to demote Himself from being the crown Prince of glory to become the son of a Jewish carpenter living under Roman oppression.

It was mercy that compelled Him to kneel beside a prostitute and say, "Neither do I condemn you....Go now and leave your life of sin" (John 8:11). The merciless religious mob wanted to kill her. But the merciful Great Physician wanted to save her.

It was mercy that caused Him to place His healing hand on the rotting flesh of lepers. It was mercy that drove Him to the pool of Bethesda to heal a man who had waited thirty-eight years to be made well. It was mercy that prompted Him to raise the widow's son back to life, transforming the funeral procession into a parade of celebration.

It was mercy that caused Him to weep over the city of Jerusalem and the plight of the Jewish people. It was mercy that compelled Him to lay down His life as a ransom for many, making eternal life possible for all who believe. It was mercy that formed the words on His blood-caked lips: "Father, forgive them, for they do not know what they are doing" (Luke 23:34).

The Price of Mercy

The price of mercy is not rubies, diamonds, sapphires, pearls, gold or silver. The price of mercy is mercy.

The story is told of a boy raised in a privileged environment by loving parents. He broke the law and was sent to the penitentiary for ten years. During all that time he was too ashamed of what he had done and of the heartache he had brought to his parents even to write to them. They wrote to him many times. But each time he refused their letters. He refused to believe they could ever forgive him, ever want him to be their son.

When his sentence was up, he finally sat down, worked up all his courage and wrote them a letter. "I'll be getting out next week," he wrote. "I want to come home, but I don't know if I'm forgiven. If you want me back, tie a yellow ribbon in the oak tree beside the railroad tracks. If I see a ribbon in the tree as the train passes our farm, I'll know it's OK to come home. If not, I won't even get off the train, and you'll never hear from me again."

"I'm Going Home!"

The day finally came. All the way home he sat nervously on the train, his apprehension mounting by the mile. Would he be welcomed back or turned away forever?

The train rounded the bend and started up the grade that led past the family farm. The anxiety was unbearable. He asked the man sitting across from him, "Will you please look out the window and tell me if you see a ribbon in the oak tree beside the tracks?"

The man turned and looked out the window. "Son," he said, "there's not one ribbon in that oak tree. There are dozens of them! Hanging from every branch and every limb! There are ribbons on the barbed-wire fence, on the rose bushes near the house—there are yellow ribbons from one side of that farm to the other! What does it mean?"

"It means," the young man shouted as he jumped from the train, "that I'm forgiven! And I'm going home!"

Happy are those who demonstrate kindness in action. Happy are those whose self-centered lives have been crushed and reshaped by the Master's hand to be full of mercy. Happy are those who restore the fallen. Happy are those whose pity is greater than their prejudice. Happy are the merciful, for they shall receive mercy.

9

Happiness Comes Through Purity of Heart

Happy are the pure in heart,
for they shall see God.

In Scripture, the heart is considered the source of the will, the intellect and the emotions. Fear and courage, love and lust, joy and jealousy, hatred and happiness, all make their habitation in the heart.

The heart is also the womb of deception. "The heart is deceitful above all things and beyond cure," says Jeremiah. "Who can understand it?" (Jer. 17:9). "From within, out of men's hearts, come evil thoughts, sexual immorality, theft, murder, adultery, greed, malice, deceit, lewdness, envy, slander, arrogance and folly," says Jesus (Mark 7:21-22).

Why we do the things we do is a mystery that the finest minds cannot explain. There are halos and horns in human nature. We have been created just "a little lower than the angels" (Ps. 8:5), but at times our thoughts and conduct are downright devilish. Locked within the heart is the divine spark to achieve the sublime. But often we do the ridiculous.

A Divine Gift

If we are to be happy in an unhappy world, Jesus teaches, we must have a pure heart. This doesn't mean we are to attain to sinless perfection, a spiritual state in which it would be impossible for us ever to sin again. Nor does it mean we must live in a monastery, looking pious and mouthing religious slogans.

A pure heart comes from God. "I will give you a new heart," the Lord says, "and put a new spirit in you; I will remove from you your heart of stone and give you a heart of flesh" (Ezek. 36:26).

We can't gain a pure heart by our own efforts. Our generation has been told to think positively. There is certainly much value in having a positive mental attitude. But there is also a great deception if we tell ourselves, My thoughts are positive—therefore my heart is pure.

Our hearts can't be made right with God through any mental process. A pure heart is the result of a divine miracle made possible by the will of God through the death of Christ on the cross. It happens when we are born "not of natural descent, nor of human decision or a husband's will, but born of God" (John 1:13).

Vertical and Horizontal

We all want what comes from having a pure heart: happiness. But how many of us are willing to go through the painful process of change that makes it possible to be happy in an unhappy world?

We must marvel at the genius of Jesus' principles of happiness. Here are precise steps with predictable results guaranteed by God to produce genuine, lasting happiness. The first four deal with man's relationship to God; the last four deal with man's relationship to man.

The message? Our relationship to other people is as vital to our happiness as is our relationship to God. Happiness has a horizontal dimension as well as a vertical dimension. We can't say, I love God, and not love other people. It doesn't work. "For anyone who does not love his brother, whom he has seen, cannot love God, whom he has not seen" (1 John 4:20).

This is quite a challenge. After all, God is easy to love. He's perfect in every way. But the jerk next door, or the boss down the hall, or the secretary across the aisle—they're a different story!

In January we make a New Year's resolution: "I will be more understanding of others." In March we scratch that out and write, "I will try to be more patient when dealing with the incompetent people that surround me." By June we scratch that out and settle for "I will not slap anyone in the face first thing in the morning."

Purification

Imagine that the beatitudes have been grouped in stacks of four—the first through the fourth on one side, the fifth through the eighth on the other. Notice how the first principle, "Happy are the poor in spirit," relates to the fifth, "Happy are the merciful." When our stubborn, rebellious spirits have been broken, we are then able to be merciful.

Also notice how the second principle, "Happy are those who mourn," relates to the sixth, "Happy are the pure in heart." When we mourn over our sin, our hearts are purified. Purity of heart comes from having faced up to the reality of who we really are inside. It comes from having looked into the mirror of our souls, seen the unspeakable and mourned over our moral and spiritual imperfection, permitting the master potter to create a new heart within us.

Living in the Now

Being a Christian doesn't mean living an unnatural life. It doesn't mean escaping from reality. Rather it means living in the now, knowing who we are and to whom we belong. It means living with a clear definition of our problems, knowing that with God's help we can face the impossible and stand in the winner's circle. It means sailing through the stormy seas of life smiling in triumph, transforming adversity into opportunity.

By the same token, having a pure heart doesn't mean we'll be free from conflict or live a life without controversy. It won't spare us from the harsh realities of life.

Just think about Jesus. He had a pure heart, and He lived in controversy every minute from Bethlehem's manger to resurrection morning. He was born part of a despised minority. The legitimacy of His birth was questioned. He was called a drunkard, a heretic and a demonized madman by religious leaders. The state had Him put to death as an insurrectionist.

No, a pure heart won't get us out of conflict and controversy. It may well be the very thing that gets us into it.

Without Wax

We can understand purity of heart in two senses. The first meaning is to be without hypocrisy, or to be sincere. The word "sincere" comes from two Latin words. *Sin* means "without" and *cere* means "wax."

The term refers to stone statues. The one thing that could make a statue worthless was a crack in the stone. In an effort to deceive a prospective buyer, a seller might mix rock dust with wax and rub the mixture into a crack on a statue. In dim inside light, the wax made the statue appear flawless. But outside, the sun's heat would melt the wax and expose the fraud. Thus for a statue to be "without wax" meant that it was authentic, genuine, just as it appeared to be.

From time to time God, the master sculptor, places us in the heat of trial and adversity, where our contents can be tested. If we have become cosmetic Christians whose faults and defects are hidden by the wax of phony religiosity, we will be exposed as frauds. We can't pretend to be pure and get away with it.

Without Defilement

The second meaning of being pure in heart is to be cleansed, or without defilement. Only the pure will be permitted to enter heaven. The Bible says, "Nothing impure will ever enter it, nor will anyone who does what is shameful or deceitful, but only those whose names are written in the Lamb's book of life" (Rev. 21:27). Nothing unclean is going to enter heaven. And God is the one who determines what it means to be clean.

But aren't we Christians already pure by the blood of Jesus which was shed upon the cross? Yes, but we must choose to remain pure. The Bible says, "Everyone who has this hope in him [to be made like Jesus, to spend eternity with Him in heaven] purifies himself, just as he [Jesus] is pure" (1 John 3:3).

In another place it says, "Come near to God and he will come near to you. Wash your hands, you sinners, and purify your hearts, you double-minded. Grieve, mourn and wail. Change your laughter to mourning and your joy to gloom [do you see the connection here between mourning over wrongdoing and purity of heart?]. Humble yourselves before the Lord, and he will lift you up'' (James 4:8-10).

Who takes the next step? We do. It's not God's job to chase us down. It's up to us to call upon Him.

Purity Is Not Pretense

As Jesus proclaimed His principles of happiness, He was looking eye-to-eye with the Pharisees, who pretended to be pure. They were proud of their religiosity. They kept the letter of the law but their hearts were cold, hard and hateful.

They worked from the outside in, while Jesus was saying to work from the inside out. Later Jesus said to them, ''Woe to you, teachers of the law and Pharisees, you hypocrites! You are like whitewashed tombs, which look beautiful on the outside but on the inside are full of dead men's bones and everything unclean. In the same way, on the outside you appear to people as righteous but on the inside you are full of hypocrisy and wickedness'' (Matt. 23:27-28).

The Bible says, ''The Lord does not look at the things man looks at. Man looks at the outward appearance, but the Lord looks at the heart'' (1 Sam. 16:7). We can pretend to be pure outwardly, but God is recording our inward thoughts, examining our motives, and cataloging the places we go and the things we say and do. He observes the literature we read, the movies we watch, the ideas we entertain. In due time He will force us, through circumstance, to look at ourselves. Without purity, that look is extremely painful.

At War With God

An impure heart is the reason for much unhappiness. When our hearts are at war with God, there is tension, frustration, anger, confusion, bitterness, loneliness, fear and guilt. When we tell a lie, our hearts hurt. When we commit adultery or fornication, our hearts hurt. When we slander another with a barbed tongue, our hearts hurt. When our actions are dishonest, our hearts hurt.

When we've injured our hearts with such massive and prolonged abuse, the only solution is a heart transplant. Talented surgeons can give us a new physical heart. But the Great Physician can give us a new spiritual heart, without pain and without cost. Remember the words God spoke through Ezekiel: "I will give you a new heart and put a new spirit in you; I will remove from you your heart of stone and give you a heart of flesh" (Ezek. 36:26).

Purity Is Not Environmental

Americans have been duped into believing that all our troubles are because of our surroundings. The message is, If you want a superior man, create a superior environment.

Need I mention that Adam and Eve were in a perfect paradise when they rebelled against God? And, conversely, that most of the New Testament was written by Paul from a jail cell? Environment guarantees nothing one way or the other.

Once the barbers' union in Chicago decided to celebrate "Barbers' Week" by demonstrating their grooming skills to the general public. They located a derelict sleeping under a bridge and made him the object of a before-and-after project.

In the "before" picture, his full beard was matted, his hair was like a lion's mane, his fingernails like buzzards' claws. The barbers shaved him, gave him a masterful haircut, manicured his fingernails and bought him a handsome new suit. Then they took the "after" picture and published both in the newspaper. There was no doubt about it: He looked like a new man.

But the change was only on the outside. Several weeks later, a reporter followed up on the story to see what had happened to the transformed man. He was found under the same bridge, his hair and beard just as unkempt as ever, his fingernails caked with grime.

We can create as magnificent an environment as we like, but unless we change the heart it's all a waste of time. There is no change until there is heart change.

Purity Is Not Taught

Americans are also being told that superior intellect and education will produce happiness.

Now intellectual development certainly has its advantages. But it's not the answer to everything, and it certainly will not produce happiness.

America is one of the most highly educated societies on the face of the earth, yet we're rotting at the core with AIDS, drugs, alcoholism, sexual perversity, hatred, oppression and greed. We pride ourselves on our social progress. But isn't it time to admit that, while we may be in the space age technologically, we're still in the stone age spiritually?

Intellectual development doesn't produce happiness. Hooray for education—but let's really hear it for purity of heart!

Conforming to God's Holiness

The benchmark of purity is the holiness of God. Because of the holiness of God, sin isn't just wrong—it's stupid. The holiness of God guarantees that every man living below the standard of purity will be caught and sentenced. The Bible says, "Be holy, because I am holy" (1 Pet. 1:16). That's not a suggestion—that's an order. God refuses to accept anything less.

King David asked, "Who may ascend the hill of the Lord? Who may stand in his holy place? He who has clean hands and a pure heart'' (Ps. 24:3-4). The author of the letter to the Hebrews wrote, ''Make every effort to live in peace with all men and to be holy; without holiness no one will see the Lord'' (Heb. 12:14). Jesus said, ''Happy are the pure in heart, for they are the only ones who qualify to see God.''

Face to Face

Is it really possible to see God? The answer is yes. Abraham had lunch with God. Moses talked with God face to face. Paul said, ''Now we see but a poor reflection as in a mirror; then we shall see face to face'' (1 Cor. 13:12).

Will you see God face to face? If you allow God to make your heart pure by the washing of the Word and the cleansing of the crimson stream from Calvary, you will see the living God face to face. God guarantees it! Happy are the pure in heart, for they shall see God.

10

Happiness Comes Through Peacemaking

Happy are the peacemakers,
for they shall be called children of God.

The world will never be the dwelling place of peace until peace finds a home in the heart of every man and woman. The pursuit of peace has become a full-time passion for our war-torn world. Peace in the home and peace among nations will never come as long as we seek peace on our own terms, as long as we cling to the things within us that make strife inevitable.

We live in an age of anxiety. With all our scientific and technological progress, we have less peace than the cave dwellers had. Our civilized world is forever looking nervously over its shoulder, fearful of finding a nuclear mushroom cloud on the horizon announcing that our planet is about to become a massive graveyard in space.

God's Gift

When Robert Oppenheimer, who supervised the development of the first atomic bomb, appeared before a congressional committee, he was asked if there was any defense against the weapon.

"Certainly," the great physicist replied.

"And that would be...?" asked the congressman.

Oppenheimer looked out over the hushed, expectant audience and said simply, "Peace."

But there is no peace. President Kennedy created a Peace Corps. We have peace marches. Political candidates promise us peace.

Meanwhile, the armies of the world grow larger and more powerful. The thundering hoofbeats of the four horsemen of the apocalypse can be heard racing toward the bloodbath of Armageddon.

There will be no peace on earth until we have made peace with God. Peace is God's gift. Man can't manufacture it. He can't imitate it. He can't duplicate it. Some folks stare into crystal balls trying to visualize peace. Others smoke dope trying to actualize it. But the bottom line is that there is no peace without God.

We Can't Give What We Haven't Got

We can't be peacemakers if we ourselves have no peace. Have you ever noticed how hard it is to give away something you yourself don't have? When we try to be peacemakers without having peace ourselves, we make things worse instead of better.

On one of my first trips to Israel, our group from San Antonio was put on a tour bus with a group from Florida. In the Florida group were two of the most critical women I had ever met.

One day, while en route to the Sea of Galilee, these two women argued for a solid hour over whether the bus window should be up or down. One would say, "If it's down, I'll die of pneumonia." The other would reply, "If it's up, I'll die of suffocation."

Enough was enough. I stepped across the aisle and, in the heat of frustration, offered what was *not* the perfect solution. "Why don't you," I said, pointing to the first one, "put the window down until your friend here dies of pneumonia? Then," I said to her startled companion, "I promise you I will close it again until she suffocates. Maybe then we'll have some peace."

It was not my finest moment. I was trying to be a peacemaker, but I had no peace myself.

Digging Deeper

Sometimes being a peacemaker in the home requires more skill than being secretary of state at a summit conference.

A wife asked her husband, "Honey, I don't think I look thirty-five. Do you?"

"No, of course not," he replied. "But you used to!"

This is not the path to peace. This is the path to cold suppers and long, silent evenings.

Have you ever made a slip of the tongue and then tried desperately to correct it—only to dig yourself into an even deeper ditch? In an effort to preserve peace, you almost declare war.

Two friends who hadn't seen each other for several years met on the street. One asked the other, "How's your wife?"

"She's in heaven," the man replied.

"Oh, I'm sorry," the first said. Then realizing that was not the best phrase to use, he said, "I mean, I'm glad...well, what I really mean is, I'm totally surprised...er, that is...."

God's Approval

The secret of peace is locked within the lyrics of the angelic chorus we sing with such blind sentiment every Christmas. The biblical text reads, "Glory to God in the highest, and on earth peace to men on whom his favor rests" (Luke 2:14). Another way to say it would be "Peace among approved men." Peace is not born because man wills it into existence. It is born when men are approved by God. Without His approval of our lives, there will never be peace.

Peace is precious. When I spoke behind the Iron Curtain several years ago, each time I came out of the state-supported church where the services had been held, both young and old approached me with an intensity seldom seen in the West, pleading, "Tell all the people in America we want peace!" There was no questioning their sincerity. Many of them had personally experienced the tragedies and devastations of World War II.

Whether we live behind the Iron Curtain or in a Manhattan penthouse, without the peace of God we'll be miserable. We may have talent, power, fame and beauty—but without the genuine, deep-seated peace of God that passes all understanding, life will be empty and meaningless.

The By-product of Righteousness

In international terms, peace is often nothing more than the time between wars when the armies of the world are reloading. The dove of peace still finds the world covered with the flood waters of hatred and greed. In spite of the finest efforts of our most seasoned statesmen, there is still no peace. Why not?

Because peace is more than a piece of paper. It's more

than a building surrounded by the colorful flags of the United Nations. It's more than a passing desire of the human heart. Peace is the by-product of a right relationship with God. If we don't have God's approval, peace is impossible.

Feeling Good or Being Good?

Paul said, "Therefore, since we have been justified through faith, we have peace with God through our Lord Jesus Christ" (Rom. 5:1). Note the sequence. First we are justified through faith—that's God's condition—and then we have peace with God.

In the heart of every man lurks a sense of inner wrongness and a conscience that will not be silenced. Try as we might to escape it, we can't. We can try to sweep it under the rug or take it to some Shangri-la of forgetfulness. But we can never go far enough to escape ourselves. We can't drink enough alcohol, snort enough cocaine or swallow enough pills to silence our consciences.

Our society tries to dismiss the whole notion of guilt, of the need for forgiveness, of the conscience, of moral responsibility. It rejects the wisdom of God's Word and embraces the humanistic solutions of rearrangement of attitudes, situation ethics and manipulation of emotions. We seek devices to make us feel good without being good, to banish evil without quitting evil, to get peace of mind without confession of sin.

King David said, "Love and faithfulness meet together; righteousness and peace kiss each other" (Ps. 85:10). Righteousness and peace go together. We can't have one without the other. If we want to feel good, we have to be good.

Confession Brings Peace

What about you? Are you searching for peace? Then stop

fighting God. Quit trying to justify your carnal conduct. Call it what God calls it: sin.

"If we claim to be without sin, we deceive ourselves and the truth is not in us. If we confess our sins, he is faithful and just and will forgive us our sins and purify us from all unrighteousness" (1 John 1:8-9). Peace is as close as the confession of sin that separates us from God.

Aren't you tired of being unhappy? Aren't you tired of a meaningless and empty life? Aren't you tired of tossing and turning on your bed at night as though the sheets were coals of fire? Jesus is your answer. "For he himself is our peace" (Eph. 2:14).

Peace Is Found in Responsibility

There must come a time in each of our lives when we take responsibility for who we are and what we have become. We can no longer blame father, mother, boss, government or God. Happiness begins the moment we refuse to keep on playing the coward, continually in retreat from reality, and accept responsibility for ourselves.

A bum sat on a curb at a downtown intersection, watching traffic come and go. A shiny limousine pulled up to the light. Seated in back was a man in a silk suit, with glistening diamond rings on both hands and a walking cane tipped with gold. As the limo pulled away, the bum said, "There but for me go I." At least he was taking responsibility for himself.

Facing Reality

Responsibility means facing, not fleeing, the risks and challenges of life. Jesus is our example. He faced the harsh task of living life with a peace that trials could not diminish. He said, "Peace I leave with you; my peace I give you" (John 14:27). He didn't speak these words in some ivory tower of detachment. He spoke them the night before He was crucified. The cross was His assignment from the beginning of the world, and He faced that assignment with unshakeable peace.

Christianity is a call to responsibility. There is not a single utterance in Scripture about dodging or ducking the hard issues of life. We are challenged to take up our cross daily; to face and fight the giants that roar into our lives unexpectedly; to put our hands to the plow and never look back; to fight the good fight of faith; to endure to the end.

What Is a Peacemaker?

In the wild, wild West, a peacemaker was a Colt .45 revolver. Happy was the man who had a quick draw! Two hundred years later, the United States has a nuclear missile called the Peacekeeper. But what is a peacemaker? How can we describe what one is like?

• A peacemaker doesn't seek "peace at any price." Jesus, the Prince of peace, invaded the temple with a whip of cords in His hand and fire in His eyes, turning over the tables of the money-changers and sending goats, cows and preachers running in panic. He didn't learn that by reading *How to Win Friends and Influence People*. He was a peacemaker—but He didn't believe in "peace at any price."

• A peacemaker is not a compromiser. Peace that is won by compromising godly principles is not peace at all. It's cowardice. It's treason to the conscience. It's anarchy toward the courts of heaven. If we've won peace through compromising the standards of righteousness, we don't really have peace. We have only the illusion of peace.

Light Shines Only in Darkness

• A peacemaker is not an appeaser. Appeasement can

postpone confrontation, but it can never bring lasting peace. World War II was born because would-be peacemakers sought to appease rather than confront. Neville Chamberlain, the prime minister of Great Britain, flew to Germany seeking an accord with Adolph Hitler. He and the other European leaders granted Hitler's every demand.

When Chamberlain got back to England, he stepped down from the plane and confidently proclaimed, "Peace in our time." But his appeasement of Hitler only convinced the Nazi fuhrer that Europe was afraid of him. Their appeasement, far from winning peace, actually guaranteed war.

• A peacemaker functions in an atmosphere of turmoil. Many people pray for a life without conflict, without battle, without strife, without clash and collision. But how can we be peacemakers if everything is perfect all the time?

Let's stop worrying about the clashes and collisions and look at them as opportunities to serve the Lord as peacemakers. Let's quit praying for an easy life and start praying to be stronger persons. Let's build bridges to people who have isolated themselves. Let's be part of the solution, for the sake of the Lord, and not part of the problem. We are the light of the world—but we only make a difference in dark places.

Tackling Problems Head-on

• A peacemaker must be willing to confront. Nothing is settled until it's settled right. If we have a boil, we can't cure it by ignoring it. The surgeon's lance must cut it open and let the poison escape. Misunderstandings, hurt feelings and suspicions that are allowed to fester will become boils. Don't just acknowledge problems and sweep them under the rug. Attack them, and attack them now.

Some people try to avoid confrontation through manipulation or intimidation. I know husbands who intimidate their wives by yelling at them. When their wives refute their "infinite wisdom" with sound logic, their brains go into neutral and their mouths fly into overdrive.

I know wives who manipulate their husbands with tears. When a conversation gets too near the heart of the matter, they turn on the waterworks. What's the result? Peace? Not really. They've dodged genuine confrontation and left the boil unlanced.

Children of God

• A peacemaker seeks the glory of God. The Bible says, "Whatever you do, do it all for the glory of God" (1 Cor. 10:31). What is our witness to the world if we, God's children, are as vicious and unforgiving as they? We seek peace not for our sakes but for Jesus' sake, not to increase our comfort but to advance His kingdom.

• A peacemaker is free of self. If we're worried about protecting ourselves, about shielding ourselves, we can't be peacemakers. We need to go back to step one in the blueprint for happiness and let the Holy Spirit crush our prideful spirits.

• A peacemaker is one whose spirit has been broken by the Holy Spirit. He has mourned over his wrongdoing. He has taken on the meekness of Jesus. He has hungered and thirsted after righteousness. He has allowed God to purify his heart. He is ready to demonstrate that he's a child of God by being a peacemaker.

Resting Between Fights?

The absence of overt strife does not necessarily indicate the presence of peace. Some people seem to be at peace—but in fact they're just resting up between fights.

When I was a boy growing up in the country, my dad had a pair of hounds that loved to fight each other. We kept them in separate pens in order to keep the peace. One hot summer day when Dad was gone and I was bored, I walked over to the kennel and let those two hounds out of their cages to renew their acquaintance.

The moment I opened the gate, those huge dogs lunged at each other. They came together in mid-air like two magnets uncontrollably drawn to each other. A big ball of growling fur rolled across the ground. "Wide World of Sports" never saw anything like it.

Those dogs fought until they were totally exhausted. Afterward, they lay down beside each other in the deep grass, snarling. They had just enough energy left to curl their lips back over their fangs. They were too tired to fight—but they were a long way from being at peace.

I know people who live like that. They fight until they're exhausted. Then they just lie around and snarl. They're not fighting—but they're surely not at peace.

We Need Peacemakers in the Home

The American family is torn by divorce, drugs, drink, delinquency, child abuse, incest and wife-beating. Who will be brave enough to make peace in the New American Combat Zone?

I was in the county courthouse one day when an attorney friend invited me to hear the proceedings of a bitter divorce case. A father and mother were arguing violently before the judge. Standing between them was their four-year-old daughter. She glanced from parent to parent as they verbally berated each other. Finally, she reached up and took their hands in hers. Gently she brought them together. Now that's a peacemaker.

We Need Peacemakers in the Nation

Abraham interceded for Sodom and Gomorrah, asking God to spare the cities for the sake of ten righteous men. His family lived there, and his heart went out to his nephew Lot and Lot's children.

America is every bit as sin-sick as Sodom and Gomorrah ever were. We're rotting from within. Who will be a peacemaker? Abraham interceded for Sodom. Moses interceded for Israel. In a time of turmoil, the Lord said to Ezekiel, "I looked for a man among them who would build up the wall and stand before me in the gap on behalf of the land so I would not have to destroy it, but I found none" (Ezek. 22:30).

Daring to Make Peace

Peace will not come to us, our homes or our country by accident. It will come when we dare to be peacemakers. When God the Father looks down from the balconies of heaven and sees one of us making peace, He looks at the angels and says, "That's My child. He's like Me. He's willing to suffer, to dare to be a peacemaker, to help bring about happiness in an unhappy world."

Happy are the peacemakers, for they shall be called children of God.

11

Happiness Comes Through Persecution

Happy are those who are persecuted
for righteousness' sake,
for theirs is the kingdom of heaven.

This is the eighth of Jesus' principles for finding happiness in an unhappy world. The first four deal with what God wants to do in us.

- Happy are the poor in spirit.
- Happy are those who mourn for their sin.
- Happy are the meek.
- Happy are those who hunger and thirst for righteousness.

The next three reveal what comes out of us because of what God has done within us.

- Happy are the merciful.
- Happy are the pure in heart.
- Happy are the peacemakers.

Our Reward

Now we come to the bottom line. How does the world receive us? One would think that a world saturated with violence, hatred and greed would be overjoyed to meet a bunch of merciful, meek, pure-hearted peacemakers.

Not so! What is the grand and glorious result of living a vibrant Christian life? The result of living a victorious Christian life in a world gone berserk is...persecution. Paul wrote, "Everyone who wants to live a godly life in Christ Jesus will be persecuted" (2 Tim. 3:12). Jesus didn't just predict persecution; He promised it: "No servant is greater than his master. If they persecuted me, they will persecute you also" (John 15:20).

The Marks of Persecution

When God gathers all His children in heaven, they will bear the marks of persecution. There will be the apostles who were beheaded, boiled in oil, burned at the stake, crucified upside down. There will be the believers who were covered with pitch, fastened to a stake and set afire to light Nero's gardens. There will be the millions murdered in cold blood by their communist captors for their testimony. Missionaries from around the globe who were slaughtered by those they were trying to win for Christ will walk heaven's streets of gold. The history of the church is soaked through with the blood of believers.

Even today, in the civilized Western world, the church of Jesus Christ suffers persecution from the secular humanist culture. The words of the tongue—especially when magnified by the media—heal more slowly than the wounds of the sword. A person's influence and godly character can be assassinated by the media as effectively as by a gangland execution.

A Clash of Kingdoms

A clash of two supernatural kingdoms rages on the battlefield of earth. It is a battle for survival between the kingdom of light and the kingdom of darkness. The kingdom of light is led by God the Father, Son and Holy Spirit with Their host of heavenly angels. The kingdom of darkness is led by Satan and the demonic powers and principalities that obey his every command.

Paul alerted us to this fact, saying, "For our struggle is not against flesh and blood, but against the rulers, against the authorities, against the powers of this dark world and against the spiritual forces of evil in the heavenly realms" (Eph. 6:12).

The clash of the kingdoms began on the first Christmas morning, when God's own Son launched His invasion of planet Earth at Bethlehem. He didn't come to pursue "peaceful coexistence" with Satan. He came to destroy him. The Bible says, "The reason the Son of God appeared was to destroy the devil's work" (1 John 3:8). The angels' announcement of Jesus' birth was a formal declaration of war against the devil.

The Decisive Victory

The final battle for the souls of men began in the sobs of Gethsemane. Arrested, falsely accused, tried and convicted illegally, Jesus was flogged mercilessly for our healing. He knew the pain of persecution.

On a windswept hill called Calvary, just outside the walls of Jerusalem, hell made its final attack—and lost. When the Son of God bowed His head and mustered His last ounce of strength to say, "It is finished," the legions of hell quaked in terror.

He descended into the bowels of the earth, looked Satan

eyeball to eyeball and introduced Himself as the lion of the tribe of Judah, the conqueror from Calvary, the Son of the living God. He ripped the gates of death and hell off their hinges and led the Old Testament believers into paradise. Now, today, the gates of hell cannot prevail against us, because the Prince of glory has defeated Satan and his demonic forces forever.

The Enemy of God's People

Two thousand years have passed. Still the battle between God and Satan rages on earth. Satan's purpose is "to steal and kill and destroy" the inhabitants of earth (John 10:10). It's his revenge for his expulsion from heaven and his defeat at Calvary. Knowing he is doomed to an eternity in hell, he does his utmost to drag those whom God created into the abyss with him.

Among his weapons for destroying the church and the children of God are persecution, slander, character assassination, ridicule, suspicion, confusion and lying. He is the father of lies. Those who follow him lie at his bidding. They are enemy agents in our midst, whose purpose is to destroy the unity of the faith and sabotage the peace of God's people.

For Righteousness' Sake

Notice that Jesus says, "Happy are those who are persecuted for righteousness' sake." He doesn't say, "Happy are those who are having a hard time in their Christian life because they try at all times to be as difficult as possible."

He doesn't say, "Happy are those who suffer because of their own poor judgment." I have known professing Christians who had rotten dispositions, made foolish decisions and used poor manners—and then thought people were opposing them because of their stand for Jesus. But it wasn't their righteousness that was bringing them grief; it was their lack of goodness.

A Poor Advertisement for the Gospel

Jesus doesn't say, "Happy are those who are scorned because they are overzealous and overbearing." Some people go to church and shout "amen" louder than everyone else, thinking it proves how spiritual they are. In reality, it only proves they have a loud mouth and the disposition of an exhibitionist. They make themselves the center of attention instead of Jesus.

Jesus doesn't say, "Happy are those who turn others off because they're such busybodies." Peter warns, "If you suffer, it should not be as a murderer or thief or any other kind of criminal, or even as a meddler" (1 Pet. 4:15). If we stick our noses in someone else's business and get them cut off, that's not persecution. We had it coming.

Shabby Christians are a poor advertisement for the gospel. Paul chided the Romans because "God's name is blasphemed among the Gentiles because of you" (Rom. 2:24). As he wrote to Timothy, we should instead "set an example...in speech, in life, in love, in faith and in purity" (1 Tim. 4:12).

Jesus Was Persecuted

Why do the righteous suffer persecution? Because goodness always provokes opposition from a fallen world.

Consider Jesus. He was meek. He was merciful. He was loving. He was a peacemaker. He was without sin. Yet He was persecuted and finally murdered.

How did the Jerusalem *Gazette* treat the Son of God? The headline screamed, "Jesus Found Guilty of Treason!" The article read, "Jesus of Nazareth is being labeled a blasphemer, a heretic, a liar, a glutton and a drunkard by local religious leaders. In worship services yesterday, He was allegedly 'casting out evil spirits.' But confidential sources close to the controversial evangelist say He is Himself demonized. Local courts have pronounced Jesus guilty of treason for inflammatory statements directed against the establishment.''

Persecution sent Jesus to the cross.

Paul Was Persecuted

Consider as well the apostle Paul. He lived the most godly and productive life in the New Testament, apart from Jesus. His pen wrote most of that mighty manuscript. Yet the more he preached Christ, the more he was beaten and sent to jail.

He was chased from city to city by stone-throwing mobs. After one stoning, his blood-soaked body was left for dead. He was lashed to the point of death with the Romans' cat-o'-nine-tails on three different occasions. At age sixty-four, in the darkness of Nero's rat-infested, disease-saturated dungeon, he penned the words that would encourage millions: "I have fought the good fight, I have finished the race, I have kept the faith" (2 Tim. 4:7).

The sharp sword of the executioner ran red with Paul's blood. His head fell into a wicker basket. He loved, he served and he gave his all. He built, he wrote and he blessed the world. He changed the course of human history with the message of the gospel.

And what was the world's reaction to his noble and magnificent contributions? "Kill him! Get that gospel-spouting troublemaker out of the way once and for all!" It was Paul who had warned us that "everyone who wants to live a godly life in Christ Jesus will be persecuted." That includes me. It includes you. It includes our churches.

Different for Jesus' Sake

A genuine Christian provokes opposition because he is different. We don't fit in. Our speech is different. Our attitudes are different. We've changed from hateful and vindictive personalities and discovered the blueprint to happiness in meekness, mercy and peacemaking. Our differences make us hated by the carnal world which is controlled by Satan.

• Abel was murdered by Cain because he was different.

• Joseph was sent to prison for refusing to have sex with the boss's wife. That was different!

• The three Hebrews refused to bow to the idol of Nebuchadnezzar when the masses of humanity didn't dare defy the king's order. They were different!

• Daniel preferred to be sent to the lions' den than to give up his morning prayer time with the true God. He was different!

• Jesus was different, as we've seen. Paul was different, too.

The question is, are *we* different from the world around us? If the apostles came back from their graves to fellowship with us, would they have to backslide to do the things we do? If we were on trial for being Christians, would there be enough evidence to convict us? We don't want to be different for its own sake. We want to be different for Jesus' sake.

Turn on the Switch!

The vital Christian arouses opposition because he is a standing rebuke to the selfishness and sin of those around him.

Jesus said, "You are the light of the world" (Matt. 5:14). Every person who lives according to Jesus' powerful principles of happiness is a light in a dark place. What is our reaction to a bright light when we've been sitting in a darkened room? We recoil like a scalded dog and cry, "Turn out the light!'' In just the same way, light is painful to those who are comfortable in the darkness of sin.

We are indeed the light of the world—but only if our switch is turned on. Turn on the switch and let your light shine before men. It will create persecution, but it will also convince sinners of their need for salvation.

The Sting of Salt

Jesus also said, ''You are the salt of the earth'' (Matt. 5:13). Salt arrests corruption.

When I was a boy I developed several sores that were not healing. My mother gave me a bath in Epsom salts. It burned like fire! I screamed, ''I'm better! I'm better!'' But my mother said, ''Get back in there.'' The salt dried up the sores. But while it was happening, I had only one desire: to get out of there!

Believers are like salt to those around them. Their presence in a society covered with sores is painful. The desire of the corrupt flesh is to get the salt out of there. Persecution is one way to drive believers away and create a carnal comfort zone.

Running Interference

The Christian arouses persecution because he interferes. He interferes with prejudices. He interferes with the freedom of lewd humor. He interferes with sinful pleasures. The Christian will not go along with the flow. He just doesn't fit in with the carnal crowd.

Christian ethics sometimes even dare to interfere with the sacred cow of business. When Jesus went into the temple and turned over the tables of the money-changers, they were mad as hornets! That very afternoon they entered into a conspiracy to kill Him.

Paul had his clothes torn off and was thrown into jail at Philippi for interfering with the business of some slave owners. A mob at Ephesus tried to tear him limb from limb because his Christian principles were ruining their business. They were getting rich making statues of the goddess Diana. When Paul preached against idolatry, the people listened—and the rich suddenly faced poverty. Their solution? Kill Paul!

Rejoice in Trials

When persecution comes—and it will—what will we do? When people lie about us, what will we do? When the media blast our churches, what will we do? When a world driven by lust and greed reviles us for righteousness' sake, what will we do?

Jesus recommends that we rejoice and be exceedingly glad. Laugh out loud. Don't mope and whine. Go home, burst through the door with a smile on your face and say, "Sweetie, they're lying about me again!"

Jesus says, "Congratulations!" In being persecuted we join the distinguished company of the prophets and martyrs who went before us. We are following in their footsteps. Persecution is living proof that we are members in good standing of the kingdom of heaven and have become a threat to Satan and his kingdom.

Think about it: Satan never turns his guns on spineless wimps. Why waste the ammunition? Satan has the casual, conditional Christians on retainer. They're his best decoys. He only turns his guns on his tormentors. When you find yourself looking down the barrel of his persecution pistol, rejoice to be in such good company.

A Path to Growth

Persecution is a path to spiritual growth. It is in the midst of struggle that our strength and endurance are developed.

When we feel we have no strength to take another step, we can say with the psalmist, "The Lord is the stronghold of my life" (Ps. 27:1).

When Satan's forces batter us through persecution, we can lift up our voices and shout, "The one who is in us is greater than the one who is in the world!" (see 1 John 4:4).

When our burdens are more than we can carry, we can simply cast all our anxiety on Him, because He cares for us (see 1 Pet. 5:7).

We can never be defeated, for "in all these things we are more than conquerors through him who loved us" (Rom. 8:37).

The Shaking of the Church

Persecution purifies the church. It drives out the spiritual cowardice, the faint-heartedness, the "conditionalness." It draws us "out of the closet." The first-century church was a persecuted church. The persecution called forth the lion-hearted. May it happen again!

Do you know what is going to bring the church of Jesus Christ into unity? Persecution! We are going to see it in these United States before Jesus returns for His bride. Get ready for the greatest shaking of the church since the first century. It's coming.

The Fire of Truth

Persecution is the wind that spreads the fire of truth. When persecution swept through Jerusalem, the Christians scattered abroad and preached the gospel everywhere. First-century persecution fanned the flames of missionary zeal until it set the world on fire.

The winds of persecution are blowing in our day. They

are only a faint breeze where many of us live. But they'll reach gale force before the Lord's glorious return. It won't ruin the church—it will revive the church.

Standing Fast

Are we willing to endure persecution? We'll never find happiness unless we live out the principles of Jesus in a way that provokes opposition and scorn from the fallen world around us.

May the Lord ignite His flame in our hearts that we may stand fast in the day of adversity and rejoice forevermore. Happy are those who are persecuted for righteousness' sake. The kingdom of heaven is theirs!

12

Happiness Comes Through Criticism

*Happy are you when men revile you and
say all manner of evil against you.*

Jesus comes to the summation of His Magna Carta of Happiness by showing us the secular world's reaction to those who live by His principles. What does Jesus promise will happen to us if we are

- peacemakers in a world at war?
- pure in heart while surrounded by corruption?
- merciful in a world without pity?
- righteous in a sin-saturated society?
- meek while everyone else looks out for number one?

In the last chapter we saw that our reward is persecution. Now Jesus expands on this theme, broadening it to include the far more common everyday experience of criticism. If we are going to be happy in an unhappy world, it's vital that we learn both how to respond to criticism redemptively and also how to avoid being bearers of negative criticism.

The Critic

There are three ways to avoid criticism: say nothing, do nothing and be nothing. The person who is never criticized is probably not breathing.

We're all interested in criticism because we all get criticized at one time or another. Part of the reason for that is that so many of the people around us are critics.

A critic is someone who has divorced hope and married despair. When he begins his conversation by saying, "I hope you won't mind my telling you this," you can be sure you will.

It never works to say anything good to a person infected with a critical spirit. Wish them a nice day and they snap back, "Don't tell me what kind of day to have!"

The critic has no dreams. He just rehearses defeats. He never sees opportunities, just obstacles. He knows no delight, no joy and no peace. He looks to find fault in other people as though it were buried treasure. He's convinced others have all the advantages, and he has only disadvantages.

Criticism Is Addictive

Criticism is like opium or liquor: it's addictive. It produces an insatiable appetite for more of itself. The more we criticize, the more we feel driven to criticize.

A conscientious wife tried very hard to please her husband, but she always seemed to come up short. He was especially cantankerous at breakfast regarding his eggs. If they were scrambled, he wanted them poached. If they were poached, he wanted them scrambled.

One morning the wife had a stroke of genius. She would

poach one egg and scramble the other. She set the plate before her grumpy husband, eagerly awaiting the praise that was, at long last, sure to come. He peered down at the plate, then at her, then at the plate, then back at her. Finally he spoke: "Can't you do *anything* right, woman? You scrambled the wrong egg!"

Learning From Our Critics

Not everyone who criticizes us is demented, deranged or demonized. Our critics are often right. The successful—and happy—person is the one who can lay a firm foundation for future success with the bricks that his critics have tossed at him.

If we're not mature enough to take criticism, we're not mature enough to handle praise. "The trouble with most of us," Norman Vincent Peale once said, "is that we'd rather be ruined by praise than saved by criticism."

Constructive and Destructive

Just about everyone knows there are two kinds of criticism: constructive and destructive. Generally speaking, constructive criticism is when I criticize you. When you criticize me, that's destructive criticism.

Seriously, constructive criticism attacks the problem, not the person. Destructive criticism attacks the person and ignores the problem. Its venom is planted by a two-legged viper trying to crush another person's self-image, character or spirituality with a self-righteous vengeance:

"*My* daughter would never stoop to something like that."

"Your clothes look as if you slept in them."

"If you were *really* spiritual, that wouldn't have happened to you."

"You're a cold, distant person."

To Restore or Tear Down?

Constructive criticism seeks to restore. Destructive criticism seeks to tear down. Remember the account recorded in John 8 of the woman caught in the act of adultery? The Pharisees wanted to kill her. But Jesus found a way to restore her. When something within us wants to hurt another person with our speech, we can be sure it's the voice of evil trying to use our tongues to do its dirty work.

Constructive criticism is a mother patiently showing her little son how to use his knife and fork: "Honey, let me show you how to cut your meat the right way." She's attacking the problem, not the person. Destructive criticism sounds more like this: "You eat like a pig! You're just like your father." The person has been attacked, the problem ignored.

Constructive criticism says, I may not like what you do, but I like you. Destructive criticism is designed from the outset to hurt, to create self-doubt, to foster suspicion. It's one of Satan's favorite weapons for destroying friendships, marriages and churches.

Slanderous Sharing

Too many Christians have mastered the heinous art of slandering one another under the banner of sharing. The ministry of slanderous sharing often begins when unsupervised prayer groups gather 'round the coffee pot and start talking:

"I drove past Bill's house last night," reports Deacon Blab. "It's up for sale."

"Oh, really?" croons Suzie Tellmemore.

"Yes," sighs Blab. "He and his wife have separated. Another woman is involved, I hear." By now the sharks are circling, smelling blood in the water.

"Wasn't his son arrested the other night in the drug bust

146

up at the high school?'' probes Brother Gab.

"You know, I just *knew* Bill was being too lenient with that boy," says Blab. "He was bound to come to no good."

"Bill really needs our prayers," someone drones as they reach for more coffee and move on to the next victim.

Speaking Truth in Love

The truth is, Bill and his son have been slandered by fellow believers under the self-righteous umbrella of sharing. This kind of conduct is shameful. Jesus warns us that "men will have to give account on the day of judgment for every careless word they have spoken. For by your words you will be acquitted, and by your words you will be condemned" (Matt. 12:36-37).

There are times when unpleasant truth does have to be told. Here are four common-sense questions to ask in handling these difficult situations:

- Is what I'm about to say absolutely true?
- Is it absolutely necessary to tell it, to this audience, at this time, under these circumstances?
- Is it fair to all concerned?
- Is my motive in telling it pure?

Cutting the Cord

If Jesus promised that criticism would be the result of living a godly life in a godless society, why should we be so surprised and upset when it comes? One reason is that many of us were raised with the notion that we must please everyone at all times.

What rubbish! Jesus was the Son of God. He was absolute perfection in human flesh. He couldn't please everyone, and neither can we.

I know forty-year-old people who are still trying desperately to accommodate the unreasonable demands of their parents. When their parents criticize them for not being attentive enough, they go into a funk. Scripture says that we are to *leave* our parents and become part of the new family created when we get married (Matt. 19:5). I believe the same principle applies to single adults who have left home and set out on their own.

Certainly it's right to honor our parents. But it is unscriptural to let them dominate our lives. We must cut the umbilical cord and close the door to continued criticism designed to manipulate us, our spouses and our children.

Father-pleasers

Destructive criticism will lose its hold on us when we decide to become Father-pleasers instead of people-pleasers. If we're still in the latter group, we're on a one-way street to a padded cell.

It is simply impossible, as Abe Lincoln said, to please all the people all the time. The very folks who praise us today will curse us tomorrow. When Jesus rode into Jerusalem on a donkey, people praised Him as the coming Messiah. When He failed to live up to their expectations of crushing Rome, they cursed Him and screamed for His blood.

People change their moods, their motives and their methods. If we allow ourselves to play the coward and compromise our principles to satisfy the momentary whim of the herd, we'll never live a single happy day. We'll always be like puppets dangling on the end of a string, with no control over our lives.

How do we face criticism? If it's untrue, disregard it. If it's unfair, keep from losing composure. If it's ignorant, smile. If it's justified, learn from it.

The Tongue

How do we keep from becoming a source of destructive criticism? This requires that we look at what Scripture has to say about our speech.

The tongue is a boneless monster that hides behind a wall of enamel waiting to lash out at its victim. It weighs less than six ounces, but it can crush and kill.

James paints a vivid portrait of the uncontrolled tongue:

> The tongue is a small part of the body, but it makes great boasts. Consider what a great forest is set on fire by a small spark. The tongue also is a fire, a world of evil among the parts of the body. It corrupts the whole person, sets the whole course of his life on fire, and is itself set on fire by hell.

> All kinds of animals, birds, reptiles and creatures of the sea are being tamed and have been tamed by man, but no man can tame the tongue. It is a restless evil, full of deadly poison (James 3:5-8).

Set on Fire by Hell

From time to time we watch on television as massive forest fires rage out of control, firefighters helpless to stop the devastation. Homes, businesses, schools, churches and millions of dollars in timber are lost.

So it is with the tongue. It is Satan's tool for destroying homes, marriages, friendships and churches.

The tongue can defile the body of Christ. Show me a divided church, and often as not I'll show you the fruit of unbridled tongues. The tongue is "set on fire by hell." The Bible tells of only two sources of fire for the tongue. It can be set ablaze with the fire of the Holy Spirit (Acts 2), or it can be set on fire by hell. The choice is ours.

Words: Transcripts of the Mind

Words! They're as common as blossoms on a spring day. Yet how mighty their power and how irrevocable their influence!

Words are the transcript of the mind. A man's words are an index of his character. Jesus said, "Out of the overflow of the heart the mouth speaks" (Matt. 12:34).

Solomon wrote, "The tongue has the power of life and death" (Prov. 18:21). If we use our tongue properly, it brings life. If our tongue is unbridled, it can deal out death.

The verse in Proverbs goes on to say that "those who love it [the tongue] will eat its fruit." If our speech is filled with criticism, bitterness, fault-finding and resentment, our future is apt to be flooded with the same.

Guarding the Tongue

The Bible says the first area of our lives that should reflect the presence of God is our speech. King David wrote, "Whoever of you loves life and desires to see many good days, keep your tongue from evil and your lips from speaking lies" (Ps. 34:12-13).

I often joke that some of us should stop asking God for power to raise the dead and start asking Him for power to close our mouths.

"He who guards his mouth and his tongue," the Bible says, "keeps himself from calamity" (Prov. 21:23). "Calamity" is a strong word. It means to be stricken physically, financially, emotionally and mentally—to be utterly and completely ruined. Many Christians suffer calamity because their tongues are out of control and God is letting them eat the fruit of it. They may be saved, but they're certainly not happy.

When we're not feeling well and we go to the doctor, he says, "Let me see your tongue." His trained eye can spot the diseases of the body through the evidence of the tongue.

When we come to God in prayer, He says, "Let Me see your tongue." He can spot the stains of criticism, of fault-finding, of gossip and slander.

Words Once Spoken...

The story is told of a peasant who had slandered several of his friends. Knowing he must repent, he went to his pastor. "I want to get right with God because of my harsh words," he said.

The minister told him, "Go fill a large sack with goose feathers. Then go around town and place a feather on the doorstep of each house where you unjustly criticized someone. Then come back here to me."

The peasant did as he was told. He took the largest sack he could find and filled it with fine, fluffy goose feathers. He obediently placed them on the doorsteps of the homes where his unruly tongue had taken its toll. He then returned to the minister's house.

"What shall I do now?" he asked.

"Go and collect all the feathers you placed on the doorsteps," said the pastor, "and bring them to me."

The peasant went out and searched frantically for the feathers, but could find not a one. The wind had carried them away. He returned to his minister and said, "Pastor, the feathers are hopelessly scattered to the four winds!"

"So it is with your critical words," said the minister. "They are easily dropped. But you can never get them back once they are spoken into existence."

We should only criticize when we can do so with justice, with kindness and with humility, for the purpose of solving a problem and not attacking a person. To criticize in any other way is to hurt others and ourselves.

In the same way, we should learn to ignore some criticism

and to welcome others. In doing so, we will take an adversity and convert it to an asset, and learn more deeply how to be happy in an unhappy world.

13

Happiness Comes Through Death

Happy are the dead who die in the Lord from now on;
they will rest from their labor, for their deeds
will follow them.

Sixty years have passed since the Sermon on the Mount with the eight beatitudes was given by the Son of God. John, who sat on the grassy slopes of the Sea of Galilee as a disciple and heard the initial utterance of Jesus' Magna Carta of Happiness, is now on the isle of Patmos, enduring persecution and writing the last book of the Bible.

John writes, "I heard a voice from heaven" (Rev. 14:13). It was a voice he knew well. It was the voice of the healer, the miracle worker, the teacher from Nazareth with whom he had lived night and day for more than three years.

The voice of Jesus was saying, "John, I want to add a postscript to the principles I gave that day by the Sea of Galilee.

I want to give another principle that will give all humanity a reason to be happy in an unhappy world. Write this down for all men and women of every age to come: 'Blessed are the dead who die in the Lord from now on' '' (Rev. 14:13).

Happy, Jesus says, is the man who dies in the Lord. He is to be envied. Can we really find happiness in death? The answer is an unshakable yes.

The Last Enemy

While I was writing this book, my beloved father, William B. Hagee, was fighting against the last enemy we all will face: death. His fight ended one afternoon in a hospital room in Houston, Texas.

That morning I knew, as my airliner plowed through the turbulence toward Houston, that this would be the last day I would ever see my father alive. My mind tumbled back in time, remembering life with my father.

Dad had faithfully served the Lord for fifty years as an ordained minister in the Assemblies of God. He was a lover of God's Word, a lover of the sheep he pastored, a lover of his family. He was a man of absolute determination. He served God with all his heart, soul, mind and strength. He ran the race of life with endurance, that he might please the Lord who had called him to be a soldier in His army.

Gathering Together

Just two months before, I had gone to visit him and been shocked to see he had lost fifty pounds in less than a month. The doctors confirmed our worst suspicions: Dad had a massive and untreatable stomach cancer. Clearly his remaining days were limited.

I felt the plane shudder and heard the wheels screech as we landed in a dense fog at Houston. Almost mechanically,

I made my way through the terminal, down the stairs and out to the taxi stand. This was a ritual I'd been through many times the past two months.

My mother was in the room when I arrived at the hospital. She had been by Dad's side night and day for two months. Her face was drawn from the physical and emotional strain. My two younger brothers were also there. We immediately did what we'd been doing since childhood. We gathered around Dad's bed for family prayer.

My heart felt as though it would break as I saw the most powerful man I'd ever known gasping for his every breath. After the prayer Dad opened his eyes and looked directly at me, as though he wanted to say something but couldn't. "How's it going, Dad?" I asked. He flipped his hands palms upward, his sign for frustration. Then he lay his head back on the pillow, closed his eyes and drifted off to sleep. That little gesture with his hands was to be the last communication we would have from Dad on this earth.

A Final Prayer

As the hours dragged by, the reality began to settle on us that this man we loved so dearly was about to die. We gathered around the bed for a final prayer. It was the most emotion-laden moment of my life. I didn't just cry. I sobbed my heart out.

I placed my hand on Dad's forehead and prayed from the depths of my soul. "Heavenly Father," I began, "as far as our earthly minds can know, as far as our limited vision can see, we gather to pray as a family for the last time on this earth.

"We praise You, Lord, for the godly life of our father. We thank You for fifty years of gospel ministry that has seen thousands of people receive Jesus Christ as Savior and Lord. We thank You for Dad's seventy-five years of vibrant life. We thank You for the good times we had together as a family.

We thank You for the way his life shaped ours.

"Heavenly Father, we commit Dad into Your tender care until we meet again around Your throne in glory. He has fought the good fight. He has finished the course. Now it's time for him to receive the crown of eternal life. Send Your angels into this room to escort him home and welcome him into the New Jerusalem that You have prepared for those who love You. We place him now in Your loving hands. In Jesus' name, amen."

We stood around the bed, weeping quietly. Our tears knew no limit. I hugged my mother and my brothers, and we kissed Dad one final time. Fifteen minutes later, he breathed his last.

Dad's death brought some life-changing lessons into focus for me. In this chapter I'd like to share them with you.

The Common Denominator

Death is the common denominator of mankind. Presidents and paupers, the rich and the ragged, the powerful and the pitiful—all die. The Bible says, "Man is destined to die once" (Heb. 9:27).

We try to deny the reality of death. Nowhere is this more evident than in our obsession with the body beautiful. Books promise us eternal youth. Exercise videos pledge renewed vigor. Television shows tell us how to look young, stay trim, keep healthy and live longer.

We buy expensive creams and rub them into our wrinkled bodies, trying to bring back the bloom of youth. We buy color-coordinated jogging suits and computer-designed running shoes. We join fancy athletic clubs and use exotic exercise machines. We go on outrageous diets. All this is just an obvious attempt to cling to this present world, to delay the aging process, to push back the signs that death draws nearer with each passing day.

The brutal truth is, we can swim in skin cream, jog every

day through rain and sleet, wear athletic togs that make us the envy of the subdivision, eat health foods three times a day—and there is still a time when we are destined to die. We have an appointment with death—one we can't cancel.

No Guaranteed Contracts

How do we manage to overlook the one obvious fact of human history, that all men and women die? The Bible certainly makes it clear enough. "What is your life?" writes James. "You are a mist that appears for a little while and then vanishes" (James 4:14).

I have talked with thousands of people concerning their eternal destiny. Most of them say, "I'm not going to die anytime soon." But not one of us has a guaranteed contract that promises we'll see the sun rise tomorrow. "Do not boast about tomorrow," the Bible warns, "for you do not know what a day may bring forth" (Prov. 27:1).

The Choice Is God's

Some Christians practice a deceptive game of religious denial concerning the inevitability of death. On many occasions I have seen Mr. and Mrs. Cheerleader walk into a hospital room and say to a terminally ill patient, "Praise God! This is the day you walk out of here!" Even worse are such cruel, ignorant and unscriptural statements as, "If you were in the will of God, this wouldn't be happening to you."

Get it straight: God heals but He doesn't choose to heal every time. Jesus walked up to the pool of Bethesda, surrounded by sick people waiting for an angel to stir the waters so they could plunge in and be healed. Jesus healed one man who was unable to step into the waters—and then slipped away into the crowd (John 5:1-16). God is sovereign. He may choose to heal someone, or He may choose to receive them into His glory. The choice is His, not ours.

Accepting Reality

Relatives who have just heard that their loved one is terminally ill may practice denial. Often when I stand with a family as the doctor candidly states that their loved one is going to die, they wait until he leaves and then say angrily, "That's just his opinion! Let's get a doctor in here who knows his business!" I encourage getting second opinions. But I also lovingly encourage the acceptance of reality.

Plain Speaking

Friends of terminally ill patients may also participate in a subtle form of denial. Under the guise of sparing them, they talk about everything except what the patient needs (and often inwardly wants) to talk about.

My cousin told me about a friend of hers who was diagnosed as having terminal cancer. At first Polly and the inner circle of friends kept the conversation light and positive.

But at one point Polly said to her friend, "We've been unfair to you. Tell us what *you* feel, what *you* want to talk about."

The woman sobbed, "Help me! I don't know how to die. I've never done it before!"

There is a delicate balance when talking to persons who are terminally ill. We must gently follow their lead. If they are in deep denial, we must be loving, patient and prayerful. The harsh reality may take some time to sink in.

But if they want to discuss the reality of death, we mustn't play the coward and duck the issue. We should graciously listen and comfort them with the Scripture. When words fail, a kiss or gentle hug may be the most eloquent statement that could be made.

Born Into Eternity

We fear what we do not understand. When a baby is in the womb of its mother, it lives in an ideal environment created by the genius of God. Its every need is met instantly. It lives in absolute comfort and tranquility.

At the moment of birth, the baby is forced to leave that perfect environment to begin an adventure called life on earth. The baby is born screaming and protesting, even as the mother and father rejoice at the new arrival.

Dying is how we are born into eternity. Death is the gateway to the life to come. Life on earth is far from an ideal environment. But it's all we know, and we cling to it tenaciously. In God's time, we will each be forced to pass from this dimension of life into the next.

We fear it. We scream, we cry and we protest. But just on the other side of the veil, God the Father is rejoicing with the angels, because one of His precious children is coming home.

The Scout's Report

When Christopher Columbus set sail, the fearful told him that the world was flat and that he'd fall off the edge of the planet into the abyss. Rejecting fear, Columbus set out— and discovered a new world. When he returned to Europe he reported, "It's beautiful! Covered with fertile fields and flowing streams! Its richness defies description. And it's so vast—there's room for everyone."

As Columbus explored the new world, so Jesus Christ explored the world beyond the grave. He died and rose from death. He returned from eternity to tell us, exactly and without doubt, what eternal life is like. He said, "Do not be afraid...I am the Living One; I was dead, and behold I am alive for ever and ever!" (Rev. 1:17-18).

An Impossible Task

A child was born blind. He never saw the dazzling beauty of nature. One day his mother heard of a gifted physician whose new technique could restore sight. She took her son in for an operation. He came out of the operating room with his eyes covered with massive bandages.

Finally, many days later, the surgeon came and began to remove the bandages. When the last one was gone the little boy cried, "I can see! I can see!"

He ran to the window and looked for the first time at the beauty of a rose, of green grass, of a magnolia tree. He turned to his mother and said, "Oh, Mother, why didn't you tell me I lived in such a beautiful world?"

The mother replied, "I tried, honey. I tried. But it was a task beyond my ability."

I can present some biblical facts about heaven (taken, in this case, mostly from the book of Revelation). But like the mother trying to describe the beauty of a rose to her blind son, the task of describing our eternal home is far beyond my—or any human author's—ability.

Eternity's Two Homes

There are actually two homes in eternity. One is the home of the righteous—called heaven—and the other is the home of the ungodly—called hell. Let's first consider the place called heaven.

Jesus assures us that heaven is real. He said, "In my Father's house are many rooms; if it were not so, I would have told you. I am going there to prepare a place for you. And if I go and prepare a place for you, I will come back and take you to be with me that you also may be where I am" (John 14:2-3).

Heaven is a land of perfection, created by the architect

of the ages for the family of God. It is a city "whose architect and builder is God" (Heb. 11:10). It is a city where there is "no more death or mourning or crying or pain, for the old order of things has passed away" (Rev. 21:4).

A Land of Comfort

The first thing we will feel in eternity will be the hand of God the Father wiping every tear from our eyes. We may die suddenly, without our families standing by, without our friends to comfort us. But none of us who are members of the family of God will ever die without our heavenly Father there to comfort us and welcome us into the land of absolute perfection He has created just for us.

As we arrive in the New Jerusalem, we will notice people arriving from the north, the south, the east and the west; from every nation, tribe and tongue on earth. We will see that each side of the four-square city has three massive gates of solid pearl. On the gates are inscribed the names of the twelve tribes of Israel.

The foundation of the city has twelve layers of precious stones. As the gates swing open, we will see streets of pure gold. The city is dazzling, having no need of sun or moon or stars, for the glory of God will light the city, and the light of the Lamb of God will cause it to shine like ten thousand suns.

A Crown Awaits Us

As the gates swing wide to welcome us, God the Father will present each of us with a white stone that has each one's new name engraved on it. Just as God changed Abram to Abraham, and Jacob to Israel, so He will give us a new name that will reflect for all eternity the nature and character He had in mind when He created us.

He will place crowns on our heads. It may be a soul-winner's crown, the crown of rejoicing. It may be a crown of righteousness for those who love His appearing. It may be a crown of glory, also known as an elder's crown. It may be a crown of life, also known as a martyr's crown, for those who are slain for their witness. Or it may be a victor's crown, for those who fight in God's spiritual warfare. Whatever it is, it will perfectly complement the dazzling white robe of righteousness, without spot or wrinkle, with which God will clothe us.

The River of Life

We'll be overwhelmed by the sound of music as we enter the New Jerusalem. It is coming from the throne of God in the center of the city, where the saints of all the ages have gathered with the angels and the elders of the triumphant church of Jesus Christ. They are singing the song of the redeemed, whose words are recorded in Revelation: "Worthy is the Lamb, who was slain, to receive power and wealth and wisdom and strength and honor and glory and praise!" (Rev. 5:12).

Running through the middle of the city is the river of life. Its water is clear as crystal. It flows from beneath the throne of God and provides eternal life to everything it touches. On each side of the river are twelve different kinds of fruit trees. The fruit and the leaves of the tree are for the healing of the nations.

Our Mansion

We will see a massive avenue of pure gold leading to the throne of God. On each side are the mansions of unspeakable splendor that God has created for His children. Over the doors, in clusters of diamonds, are the names of heaven's beloved citizens. Abraham. Isaac. Jacob. Moses. David. Jeremiah and the prophets. Paul and Peter and the other apostles.

Then we will see them: the mansions with our own names over the doors. This is our eternal home. We will live here forever and ever in a perfection that our minds cannot grasp.

A Grand Reunion

Heaven is a place of reunion. As we walk toward the throne to join in the singing, our departed loved ones come running across the fields of glory, crying with delight, "You're home! You're home!"

We've all seen reunions in airports and train stations, when long-separated relatives are brought back together. But there is coming a grand reunion day unlike anything we've ever seen on this earth. Think of it: standing around the throne of God, hand-in-hand with our families for the ceaseless ages of eternity.

The Place Called Hell

All this lies in store for us—if we have joined the family of God, if we have believed on the Lord Jesus Christ and accepted Him as our personal Lord and Savior. If we haven't, we'll find ourselves spending eternity in a different place.

It too is a real place, a place of such utter horror that we can scarcely make ourselves think of it. It was set aside by God for those who reject Him as their Father and who reject Jesus as Savior and Lord. It is the place called hell.

An Inescapable Reality

"But I don't believe in hell!" you say.

Perhaps you don't—but God does. Jesus says those who don't believe will not "escape being condemned to hell"

(Matt. 23:33). He told His followers, "Do not be afraid of those who kill the body and after that can do no more. But I will show you whom you should fear: Fear him who, after the killing of the body, has power to throw you into hell. Yes, I tell you, fear him" (Luke 12:4-5).

Do I believe in a place called hell, with a literal, eternal, tormenting fire? Yes, I do. And I'm in good company. Jesus believed in it, too. He spoke of it often:

• "Anyone who is angry with his brother will be subject to judgment...Anyone who says, 'You fool!' will be in danger of the fire of hell" (Matt. 5:22).

• "If your right eye causes you to sin, gouge it out and throw it away. It is better for you to lose one part of your body than for your whole body to be thrown into hell" (Matt. 5:29).

• "The Son of Man will send out his angels, and they will weed out of his kingdom everything that causes sin and all who do evil. They will throw them into the fiery furnace, where there will be weeping and gnashing of teeth" (Matt. 13:41-42).

The Rich Man and Lazarus

In the story of the rich man and Lazarus, Jesus pulls back the curtain of eternity and lets us glimpse the other side. Both men in the story lived on earth. Both have died. Both have stepped into eternity: one into an inferno called hell, the other into a paradise of perfection called heaven.

The rich man looks up from his waterless prison into God's paradise and knows he has been a fool. In all his haste to make a fortune, he never took time to settle his account with God. He didn't live an utterly immoral life on earth. He simply left God out. He was too busy amassing money and power to be concerned about his soul.

The rich man hears the angelic choir singing around the

throne of God. But when he turns to listen to the sobs of hell's tortured legions, he knows he will have to listen to that concert of madness night and day for all eternity.

The rich man sees Lazarus being comforted in the bosom of Abraham. But he realizes that *he* will never know one second of peace or comfort.

The rich man sees the river of life flowing from beneath the throne of God. He begs for one drop—just one drop—of water for his parched tongue. On earth he could drink any amount of the most extravagant wine. But the tables are turned now. "Abraham replied, 'Son, remember that in your lifetime you received your good things, while Lazarus received bad things, but now he is comforted here and you are in agony' " (Luke 16:25).

A Hellish Reunion

There will be reunions in hell, too. Everyone who fails to accept God the Father through Jesus Christ will meet the Hitlers, the Stalins and the Judas Iscariots in hell. They will be surrounded by liars, whoremongers, murderers, sorcerers and idolaters. All of them will remember, to their everlasting torment, the opportunities they had in this life to acknowledge God. But they let them pass by.

The Ultimate Secret

Every day of our lives, we live one breath away from eternity. The most important question of life is, Am I ready to meet God?

If you are not, and you wish to acknowledge God as your Father through His Son, Jesus Christ, just pray this simple prayer and you'll become a member of the family of God, with heaven as your eternal home.

Heavenly Father, I know that I am a sinner and need

your forgiveness. I believe that Jesus died for my sins. I am willing to turn away from my sin and live a godly life. I now invite Jesus Christ into my heart as my Lord and Savior. I am willing, with God's help, from this day forward to follow Christ as Lord of my life. In Jesus' name I pray. Amen.

At this moment, you have discovered the ultimate secret of being happy in an unhappy world. It's knowing that God is your heavenly Father, that Jesus is your Lord and Savior, and that heaven is your eternal home.

Have a happy life—and a happy forever!